150 DAYS
OF
PRAISE

150 DAYS
OF PRAISE

By Delena Kay Flakes

R.A.G. Publishing

Beaumont, Texas

http://www.ragenterprise.com

CONTRIBUTORS

Thank you to all of the persons who contributed to this project. Your words have helped to make this book complete. I appreciate each of you!

Ethel D. Ellis (AKA: "Mother Ellis")

Kim Dromgoole

Gwendolyn Jones

Jennifer Goldman

Bridgett Moore

Dr. Brenda Mullin

Jessica Sebring

Roberta Sinclair

Minister Bernita Taylor

Christopher Zephyr

With the exception of those entries where the contributor is noted, all entries are authored by Dr. Delena Kay Flakes

DEDICATION

Thanks be to God for His love, His compassion, His plan and purpose for us, and His Word that guides, directs, and encourages us! His Word is truth and everlasting.

This book is dedicated to my mother, Ethel D. Ellis, my family; Garland Flakes I, Brittany, Chaundra, M'Kenzie, Garland II, Lauryn, and to my all of my *"Guest"* family members.

And, my friends; Cheryl Brown-Smith, Tracy Allen, Vicki Gates and Sandra Villasana.

DAY 1

Always Rejoice

Philippians 4:4 Rejoice in the Lord alway: [and] again I say, Rejoice.

PRAISE DAY 1--This book is for Christians! It is for those of us who are "Blood Born Believers". It is for those of us who pray and know who to praise. It is for the obedient, the giver, the servants, the meek, the humble, and the ones of us who love the Lord! This book is for us because some times, even the best of us get weary. We are worn out by our trials and we are weak because of our circumstances. Every once in a while, we just need to take a PRAISE BREAK!

No matter how long we have been in church and no matter how strong our faith is, there will be times even in the lives of us Christians when we will be pushed and stretched, challenged and persecuted to the point where we find it hard to praise the Lord. In this book, there are 150 ways and reasons to praise God, even in our trials! The enemy doesn't want us to praise God and in those times of stress and depression, we have to offer a "sacrificial" praise where we praise God when we don't *feel* like it.

Praise changes the atmosphere around us! Praise will take

our walls down! Praise will cause the troubling spirit from the enemy to vacate our space! When we praise, it changes us on the inside—something we can feel. And, it changes us on the outside—something we and others can see! When we praise, it's just like the old school days when we had P.E. (Physical Exercise). When we involve ourselves in spiritual P.E. (PRAISE Exercises), we will begin to lose weight! We will lose physical weight AND spiritual weight! Feeling a little "heavy"? Let's get our PRAISE ON!

Anybody want to join me for a PRAISE PARTY? I would say, by virtue of the fact that you are reading this book, that you are shouting a resounding "YES"! For the next 150 days, instead of praying, fasting and asking God for something, we will be singing and shouting praises to our GOD, the only One True and Living-Loving God, for what He already has done and what He already has planned for our lives! He has heard our cries and has pitied our groans, now it is time to believe by faith that we have those petitions we have prayed for! Let us REJOICE because our BLESSING is at HAND! We have the VICTORY---TODAY!!!!! REJOICE, again I say, "REJOICE"!!!

Work Sheet for PRAISE Day 1

Make a list of Christian praise songs you really enjoy! Go to the internet or get your CD's out and make for yourself a collection of 45 minutes to 90 minutes worth of praise music! Then, every morning, when you wake up, the first thing you do is turn on your Praise music!

Consider this as your P.E. which is your "Praise Exercise" as mentioned earlier! You will find that just as physical exercise causes and helps you to lose weight; your Praise Exercise will help you lose *spiritual* weight! You will be free from depression, loneliness, hopelessness, shame, guilt and more!

LIST:

1. _____
2. _____
3. _____
4. _____
5. _____
6. _____
7. _____
8. _____
9. _____
10. _____
11. _____
12. _____
13. _____
14. _____
15. _____
16. _____
17. _____
18. _____
19. _____
20. _____
21. _____
22. _____
23. _____
24. _____
25. _____
26. _____
27. _____
28. _____

DAY 2

Give Thanks

I Thessalonians 5:18 In everything give thanks; for this is the will of God in Christ Jesus for you.

PRAISE DAY 2--Thank you all for joining me for the Praise Fest! For today, let us begin by THANKING GOD for everything--and I do mean EVERYTHING-- we already have! Thank You Father for what I have today! Thank You for life, health and strength that I have TODAY, thank You for my children, my husband, my job, for the finances that I have TODAY; thank You for Your Love for me, thank You for my mother, my sisters and my brother; thank You for joy and peace that I have TODAY; Thank You for my house, the car that I drive, the clothes that I have to put on, shoes on my feet, food to eat, THANK YOU GOD, FOR EVERYTHING!!!

Not only do we want to thank Him for everything we have but even in every situation! Thank God for your job and the people on your job. Thank Him even for the ones who have a tendency to "get on your last nerve"! It's those people who remind us that we too sometimes get on God's nerves! And, it gives us reason to be more thankful because He has forgiven us, ONE MORE TIME!

We want to thank Him in a "childlike" manner! Have you ever heard children praying? They thank God for everything from the pet dog to the sun shining in the sky, from their moms and dads to their Nanas and Paw Paws. They thank God for every big and every small thing in their lives. Let us do the same and watch God move in our lives!

Think about the people, places and things you are thankful for and list them below. You will find that the more you THINK, the more you will THANK!!

LIST:

1. _____   16. _____
2. _____   17. _____
3. _____   18. _____
4. _____   19. _____
5. _____   20. _____
6. _____   21. _____
7. _____   22. _____
8. _____   23. _____
9. _____   24. _____
10. _____   25. _____
11. _____   26. _____
12. _____   27. _____
13. _____   28. _____
14. _____   29. _____
15. _____   30. _____

DAY 3

Praise His Name

I Chronicles 29:13 "Now therefore, our God, We thank You and praise Your glorious name.

PRAISE DAY 3—In Exodus 3:13, 14, Moses asked God His name. To which, God replied, "I am that I am." This *Name* of God is so simple yet so divine! Since there is no one name that can truly apply to the Person and Being of God, He simply tells Moses, "I AM". This Name encompasses two very important concepts. The first one is, "I AM" denotes a constant state of being! God's power, His essence, His existence are all constant! They are never beginning and absolutely never ending! Secondly, "I AM" indicates that God is so vast that He is indescribable and cannot be held or bound by one name! He is literally saying, by my own translations, "I am (everything) that I (say) I am"!

Can you imagine? God? He is from one extreme to the other! He has life and death in His hands! He is the Lord God Almighty, who is, who was and is to come (Revelation 4:8)!

So, today, let's just praise His Name! His promises are in His Name! Praise the Name of God our Father, El Shaddai,

Elohim, El Elyon, Wonderful, Counselor, Mighty God, Everlasting Father, King of Kings, Lord of Lords, the Beginning and the End, the First and the Last, my Shield, my Protection, my Provider! He is my peace, my joy. He is the lover and keeper of my soul! He is my EVERYTHING!! Halleluiah!

Use your Bible's resources and identify the Names of God. What Names do know Him and call Him by?

1. _____	16. _____
2. _____	17. _____
3. _____	18. _____
4. _____	19. _____
5. _____	20. _____
6. _____	21. _____
7. _____	22. _____
8. _____	23. _____
9. _____	24. _____
10. _____	25. _____
11. _____	26. _____
12. _____	27. _____
13. _____	28. _____
14. _____	29. _____
15. _____	30. _____

DAY 4

God is My Father

Isaiah 64:8—But now, O Lord, You are our Father; We are the clay, and You our potter; and all we are the work of Your hand.

PRAISE **DAY** 4--Today we are going to praise God because He is our FATHER and we are His Children! Because He is my FATHER, God has obligated Himself to take care of me, protect me, feed and clothe me, guide me, teach me, and LOVE me! As His child, all He asks of me is to LOVE HIM in return and OBEY Him (Matthew 6:9)!

Also, if I am His child, I have an obligation to Him. Think about your own parents (godly parents that is) and what they expected of you. I remember my mother always telling me, "Don't embarrass me!" and "Remember who you belong to!" She constantly reminded my siblings and me that everything we did or did not do was a reflection of her. God is the same way! If we say we are Christian, then the way we live our lives is a reflection of our relationship with Him.

Lastly, remember that God wants us to "be holy for I [the Lord] am holy," (I Peter 1:16). He has also provided us with His Holy Spirit so that we will be able to do has He commands! Thank you FATHER for loving me! Halleluiah!

What do you consider to be the characteristics of a "good father"? List them below and find the Scripture that substantiates your thought. Accept that He is "Our Father which art in heaven", and realize that you are His child.

A GOOD FATHER   **SCRIPTURE**

_____   _____

_____   _____

_____   _____

_____   _____

_____   _____

_____   _____

_____   _____

_____   _____

_____   _____

_____   _____

_____   _____

_____   _____

DAY 5

Bow Down and Worship

Psalm 95:6 Oh, come, let us worship and bow down; Let us kneel before the LORD our Maker.

PRAISE DAY 5-- I feel Him in my spirit! His breath is upon me! It makes me want to BOW DOWN AND WOSHIP HIM!!! This is the call of the Lord upon us TODAY! Let us take some TIME TODAY to BOW DOWN AND WORSHIP HIM! This is Holy Ground (our hearts)! He is God! He is Holy! He is Righteous! He sanctifies me! He makes me righteous! Bow, bow, bow down, bow down and worship HIM in the beauty of Holiness!

When we worship God, we bow down before Him, recognizing our own weaknesses. When we praise God, we armor ourselves up for the day! That is why I encourage you to praise God, first thing in the morning.

In the evenings, we should worship Him, as we are praying and/or preparing for bed. Worship acts to "decontaminate" us from the day's trouble, strife, hopelessness, the sins of the world and sins we have committed ourselves. By exposing ourselves to the presence of God, we recognize where we have sinned and we then become quick to repent and ask for forgiveness. If you want to experience a night of sweet rest as you sleep, worship the Lord, before you lay down to sleep!

Now, make a list of worship songs that you can listen to before you go to sleep:

LIST:

1. _____
2. _____
3. _____
4. _____
5. _____
6. _____
7. _____
8. _____
9. _____
10. _____
11. _____
12. _____
13. _____
14. _____

15. _____
16. _____
17. _____
18. _____
19. _____
20. _____
21. _____
22. _____
23. _____
24. _____
25. _____
26. _____
27. _____
28. _____

DAY 6

Praise Walk

Galatians 5:25 If we live in the Spirit, let us also walk in the Spirit.

PRAISE DAY 6—Walk around your walls!! Just as Joshua did in the Battle at Jericho, today while you praise, WALK! Walk around your house, walk around your job, walk around the block in your neighborhood, walk around your child's school, walk around your CHURCH (If your church isn't open, walk around the outside of the building). And, while you are walking, PRAISE GOD! Don't be afraid to give an audible praise out to Him! Put on your headphones, play your praise music, and praise your way to VICTORY!

While you are walking, call out the names of the leaders of your church. Call out the names of your pastor, pastors, and associate ministers. Praise God for His will being performed in your church. Praise breaks the yokes! Praise Him for yokes being broken, confusion being removed and for all of the souls—old and new— that are right now being saved. Praise Him for all of the souls that are coming in from the north, the south, east and west!

Invite members of your church body to walk around with you. If possible, make this a church effort. It can be done after one of your Wednesday night Bible Studies. If you have the time, walk around SEVEN TIMES! Halleluiah!!!

Write down the names of your pastor(s) and church leaders here. Call out their names as you are walking around the wall of your church.

1. _____   16. _____

2. _____   17. _____

3. _____   18. _____

4. _____   19. _____

5. _____   20. _____

6. _____   21. _____

7. _____   22. _____

8. _____   23. _____

9. _____   24. _____

10. _____   25. _____

11. _____   26. _____

12. _____   27. _____

13. _____   28. _____

14. _____   29. _____

15. _____   30. _____

DAY 7

Praise God for Others

Romans 12:15-- Rejoice with those who rejoice, and weep with those who weep. 16 Be of the same mind toward one another. Do not set your mind on high things, but associate with the humble. Do not be wise in your own opinion.

PRAISE DAY 7—Praise the Lord for someone else's victory and/or blessing! Look around you! See how God has blessed someone close to you. Who has received a promotion lately? Was it someone else? Has the Lord blessed one of your children? Has a co-worker gotten that house that he or she has been praying for? Who's getting married? The reason we want to praise God for them is because—what He's done for them, He can and will do for us! It also removes any jealousy that we may have (surprise)! God can't bless us if we are coveting someone else's blessing! Trust God to bless you also! He CAN and HE WILL! Halleluiah!!!

Who are you praying and praising God for today? There are times when we have to let go of those we have been "carrying" in our prayers and just praise the Lord! He knows this person or these people better than you do. So, today, call their names out loud as you praise Him for what He is doing in their lives!

LIST: WHO ARE YOU PRAISING GOD FOR TODAY?

1. _____

2. _____

3. _____

4. _____

5. _____

6. _____

7. _____

8. _____

9. _____

10. _____

DAY 8

Jehovah-Jireh

Genesis 22:14--**And Abraham called the name of that place Jehovah-jireh: as it is said to this day, In the mount of the LORD it shall be seen.**

PRAISE DAY 8--Praise His Name! Jehovah Jireh! The Lord _IS_ my Provider! Whenever I get discouraged, I remind myself that the Lord is still in the business of providing for His children. It is not ours to be overly concerned about the things that we cannot control. When we place our lives in His hands, know that He has our best interest at heart!

Also, know that He is in control of our lives and everything that happens to us. Our only concern is to know that we are in His will and that we are doing our best to obey His command and His will for us.

Everything you need, God already has it to provide it to you! No matter what! He owns the cattle of a thousand hills which means every now and then, I should be able to eat steak! Trust Him as you are praising HIM! HE WILL PROVIDE!

What are you believing God to provide for you today? Identify a situation where you know that it was only the Lord who provided for you at a time when you needed Him most. Write your praise report and use it to encourage you and/or to encourage someone else!

PRAISE REPORT:

_____

_____

_____

_____

_____

_____

_____

_____

_____

_____

_____

_____

_____

_____

_____

DAY 9

Jehovah-Nissi

I Corinthians 15:57 But thanks be to God, which giveth us the victory through our Lord Jesus Christ.

PRAISE DAY 9—Praise His Name! JEHOVAH-NISSI! The Lord is my Banner; the Lord is my VICTORY!!! Give God the praise HE deserves! Praise Him as if you ALREADY HAVE what you've been praying for! This praise is your VICTORY DANCE!! And, it is an element, an outward expression, a visible sign of your FAITH! Remember? Without FAITH it is impossible to please God! So GO AHEAD! DANCE! SHOUT! You HAVE the VICTORY!! Glory to GOD! Halleluiah!

PRAISE REPORT:

_____

_____

_____

_____

_____

_____

DAY 10

Write the Vision

Habakkuk 2:2 And the Lord answered me, and said, Write the vision, and make it plain upon tables, that he may run that readeth it.

PRAISE DAY 10—WRITE THE VISION! In this verse of Scripture, Habakkuk was given a vision of things to come. God instructed him to write the vision down so that those who read it would "run". God also explained to Habakkuk that the vision was for a time in the future (Hab. 2:3). The Lord assures Habakkuk that he may not see the end results immediately, but nevertheless, "thought it tarry, wait for it, because it will surely come".

Although this Scripture is referring to Biblical prophecies, we can also associate it with our lives. There are things that you have been praying about and believing God for. There may be things that you have waited for so long that you are on the verge of giving up and giving in. Just remember and be reminded that although it may seem to tarry, if it is God's will for you, it WILL HAPPEN!

So, now that we have praised GOD for the blessings we have been praying for, let us WRITE THE VISION! Those things that you have been praying and believing God for, write them down in your journal, make a vision poster and put it up in a place where you can share it with your family, especially your spouse! Everyone--on one accord! That will only happen if you WRITE THE VISION! Once you write it, continue to PRAISE THE LORD as if you already have what you've been praying for!

I know that some of you have been praying for things like a new house, a new car, or a new/better job. Don't forget things like a better relationship with Christ, increase in ministry, increase in you spiritual walk, and increase in your church. Then add those things that you have been dreaming about but you know that it will only be because of God that those things come to past! Now, SHOUT because you have the VICTORY!

Write down the things that you have been praying for! What dreams do you have? Make it plain and make a plan! (You might have to get more paper for this one). Now, give God some praise!

DREAMS AND VISIONS

_____

_____

_____

_____

_____

_____

_____

_____

_____

PLANS

_____

_____

_____

_____

_____

_____

_____

_____

_____

_____

DAY 11

Great God

Psalm 95:3 **For the LORD is the great God, And the great King above all gods.**

PRAISE DAY 11— Psalm 150:1 & 2 tell us to "Praise ye the LORD. Praise God in his sanctuary: praise Him in the firmament of his power. 2) Praise Him for his mighty acts: praise Him according to his excellent greatness." Psalm 95:3 tells us that the Lord is the great God and the great King above all gods!

When we realize how GREAT God is, we know that if He can do all that, then our petitions, problems and circumstances are NOTHING! Today, meditate on how GREAT GOD is! HE created the world and everything in it from NOTHING! He spoke the Word and it manifested! Look at God's nature around you and see—again—how GREAT He is! Praise Him! Praise God our CREATOR, our MAKER! The One who can take NOTHING and make EVERYTHING!

Think about the smallest things that we take for granted every day. The thing that I thought about today was gravity! Think about the earth spinning at 700 to 1,038 miles per hour (depending upon how far away from the equator you are). Even at that speed, we are able to stand without falling or getting dizzy. With the right amount of gravity, we can jump without fear of floating out into the atmosphere! What a mighty God we serve!

Think about something you have taken for granted all of your life. Realize now that it is only because of God that this/these things happen or exist! Write that down and let it be an encouragement for you to praise God:

PRAISE REPORT:

_____

_____

_____

_____

_____

_____

_____

_____

_____

_____

_____

_____

DAY 12

God's Mercy, Grace & Favor

II Corinthians 13:14 —The grace of the Lord Jesus Christ, and the love of God, and the communion of the Holy Spirit be with you all. Amen.

PRAISE DAY 12— Today, we will Praise God for His MERCY, GRACE and FAVOR! Too many times, we disqualify ourselves from receiving God's blessings! We think to ourselves that we have done too much in our lives to deserve blessing from God that overflow! We think that we don't pray enough, we don't fast, we don't serve Him enough, we don't read our Bibles enough. We often think that the blessing we are praying for is beyond our reach because of who we are and because of who we aren't in Christ!

Paul reminds us in the verse above that the grace of our Lord and Savior, Jesus Christ, along with the love of God, and the communion of the Holy Spirit abides with us forever! We don't have to earn His grace because we can't! Otherwise, it would not be grace or the favor of God!

Well, my brothers and sisters, just rest assured in knowing that God has given us HIS GRACE! He has given us HIS MERCY—which is new every day! And HIS UNMERITED

FAVOR—that means He blesses us even when we don't deserve it! Let us rejoice in HIS LOVE today! Halleluiah!

PRAISE REPORT:

_____

_____

_____

_____

_____

_____

_____

_____

_____

_____

_____

_____

_____

_____

_____

_____

DAY 13

God's Will Be Done

Matthew 6:10—Thy Kingdom come, Thy will be done on earth as it is in heaven.

PRAISE DAY 13— We pray, "Thy Kingdom come, Thy will be done…" (Matthew 6:10). Today, as we praise, let's THANK and PRAISE GOD for HIS WILL in our lives! Let's review our lists that we made on Day 10 and praise Him for His will being done in all of those areas we have been praying for!

Understand that when you are praying for the will of God to be done, it may not look anything like what you want to happen or how you want it to happen! If it is in God's hands, let it stay there. While you are waiting, just praise His for the work that He is doing!

Let our prayers, desires and request be purified by His will! We want everything we are praying for to be in line with God's will for our lives! He can and He WILL! Rejoice and shout out to God; "COME Kingdom of God! BE DONE will of God!" Not only in your life, but in the lives of everyone and everything on your list! Know that when we are in God's will, we have peace, we have His power, and we have HIS PRESENCE!! Halleluiah!

Where/what do you want the will of God—not yours but His—to

show up in your life? In the lives of others? Write them down here!

LORD, FROM TODAY FORWARD, NOT MY WILL BUT YOURS BE DONE!:

_____

_____

_____

_____

_____

_____

_____

_____

_____

_____

_____

_____

_____

_____

_____

_____

DAY 14

Clap Your Hands!

Psalm 47:1-- [[To the chief Musician, A Psalm for the sons of Korah.]] O clap your hands, all ye people; shout unto God with the voice of triumph.

PRAISE DAY 14—When we read the Book of Psalms and research the word "Praise", we find that there are several "levels" of praise! For today, we are going to 'TODAW'' GOD! That is, PRAISE GOD with the CLAPPING OF OUR HANDS!!! That's right! Whenever you get the feeling today, or better yet—just because—clap your hands and give God some PRAISE! Just clap! Just CLAP! Think to yourself that every time you CLAP your hands in PRAISE to GOD, you are slapping the devil in his face! Doesn't that make you want to shout right now! Go ahead! CLAP YOUR HANDS!!!

John P. Kee produced a song entitled, "Clap Your Hands" in 1997 on his album "Strength". He shared that when we think about God's goodness and kindness, we ought to clap our hands! Well, let's take it a little further. When we think about GOD, it should make us want to clap our hands.

Clapping releases tension and anxiety. Clapping multiplies

the effects of our praise! Let's just praise Him with the clapping of our hands right now! Just start thinking about His goodness. Think about all of the things He's done for you! Think about all of the things He is doing for you right now and think about all that He will do for you in the future! That is enough to make you want to clap your hands in VICTORY and shout out to God! Come on! TODAY—Praise God with the clapping of your hands!

PRAISE REPORT:

_____

_____

_____

_____

_____

_____

_____

_____

_____

_____

_____

_____

DAY 15

Surrender All

Matthew 5:4—Blessed [are] they that mourn: for they shall be comforted.

PRAISE DAY 15—There are times when mourning is necessary. Even in our praise, take time to mourn. Not only do we mourn for ourselves but, for others also. We may not be able to feel what others who are hurting may feel, but we can still mourn. We can take a moment and cry with them. We can take a moment and share in their agony. We can take time out of our day and sympathize. When we do, let us also surrender! Yes, we can worship God when we surrender ALL to HIM! We know that He can HANDLE ALL that we might come up against! While we are worshipping God and increasing our praise and our faith, the enemy will attack to get us off balance and to get us off focus. It's okay! Stop! Take a moment, and surrender all of your hurts, all of your pain, all of your tears, in a moment of SURRENDERED PRAISE! Let the healing begin!

When you take just a moment to realize that there are others who are worse off than you, you become more grateful for what you already have. This realization will cause to you praise the Lord in a surrendered position! We can say, "Lord, I'm sorry! I didn't realize how blessed I am already!" We can surrender all things to HIM! When we do, we put ourselves in position to be comforted by God.

Work Sheet for PRAISE Day 15

Identify all of the things in your life that you need to surrender to God. Also, make a list of people you know who need your prayers. As you praise, surrender all of your cares and concerns over to the Lord, knowing that He is big enough to handle your problems. Then, after you have surrendered your concerns, release the concerns of the others who are on your list.

MY CONCERNS	OTHERS TO PRAY FOR

DAY 16

The Lord is My Peace

Philippians 4:7--And the peace of God, which passes all understanding, shall keep your hearts and minds through Christ Jesus.

PRAISE DAY 16--Everyone goes through storms! It doesn't matter who we are, how old we are, how much money we have, our educational level, our skin color or our inheritance. Sooner or later we will have a storm experience! What happens to many of us is we get focused on the storm and we forget that as Children of God, we have Christ in the boat with us! We don't have to go through the storm alone. However, we do have to endure the storm.

What separates the Children of God from the rest of the World is our relationship with God! He has promised to give us His peace which is a peace that surpasses all our understanding. So when the world seems to be in a state of chaos, we can still praise because of Jehovah-Shalom! The Lord IS MY PEACE! Let's us call forth the PEACE OF GOD as we rejoice and PRAISE HIS NAME--JEHOVAH SHALOM!

As we are praising God today, let's thank Him for His peace! It is a peace that exceeds all of our expectations. It is a peace that overcomes our greatest sorrows. As we are praying, CALL out the people, place and things where you want the peace of God to reign and dwell. LET THERE BE PEACE IN THIS PLACE, THIS HOUSE, THIS CITY, THIS STATE, THIS GOVERMENT, THIS NATIONS, ALL NATIONS, IN THE NAME OF JESUS!!! AMEN AND AMEN AGAIN!

Work Sheet for PRAISE Day 16

Identify all of the people, places and things in your life where you want the peace of God to dwell! Don't forget to praise God for His peace in places where you are everyday! Rejoice in knowing that His is a greater peace that no one can take from you!

PEACE ~ PRAISE REPORT:

_____

_____

_____

_____

_____

_____

_____

_____

_____

_____

_____

_____

_____

_____

_____

DAY 17

In Due Season

Galatians 6:9-- And let us not be weary in well doing: for in
due season we shall reap, if we faint not.

PRAISE DAY 17—Praise God for your "DUE SEASON"! While the rest of the world celebrates the four seasons; spring, summer, autumn and winter, Christians also have and additional season—DUE SEASON! God recognizes it when we live for Him! He sees all that we do on His behalf! He sees our work in the garden of ministry. Let us be encouraged because God confirms that our work, our labor, is NOT IN VAIN! So, don't be weary, don't be afraid, don't give up, and don't give in! Because this is our DUE SEASON! As you praise God, today, shout out because you are about to REAP in your HARVEST!

IT'S MY SEASON! PRAISE REPORT:

_____

_____

_____

_____

_____

_____

_____

_____

_____

_____

_____

_____

_____

_____

_____

_____

_____

_____

DAY 18

God's Promotion

Psalm 75:6, 7-- For promotion [cometh] neither from the east, nor from the west, nor from the south. 7) But God [is] the judge: he putteth down one, and setteth up another.(KJV)

PRAISE DAY 18—Your promotion is at hand! Give God the PRAISE! Know that it is He who promotes you; it is He who delivers you, it is He who makes your enemies your footstool! What do you believe God for? Your increase comes from God and not man! Don't depend on man to uplift you or exalt you or promote your, or increase you! Even if God has to move someone out of the way, He can and He will—exalt you when you humble yourself. So, this day, surrender your service as unto the Lord! What God has for you, it is for you and no one can undo what God has done! HE will open doors that cannot be shut. HE will close doors that cannot be open! So, PRAISE HIM today for everything HE has for you according to His PERFECT will! In Jesus' Name we pray and praise!!

PEACE ~ PRAISE REPORT:

DAY 19

Bless the Children

Psalm 127:3 -- Behold, children *are* a heritage from the LORD, The fruit of the womb *is* a reward.

PRAISE DAY 19— Our children are a blessing from God. Good, bad or otherwise, they are still God's blessing to us! Today, let's rejoice in the Lord and bless His for our children. Let's bless Him for all children. Rejoice for all of the children in your church. Praise God for all of the children in your neighborhood. Praise God and bless the children in your city! We can praise Him for His purpose, plan and protection for every child we know and for every child we come in contact with. Today, as you are reminded of a name, praise God for that child. As you come in contact with them, lay your hand on them, tell them that they are loved, speak God's blessing into their lives, and praise God for their existence. God loves His children! And, guess what? YOU are a CHILD of the KING!!! Don't forget to thank Him for allowing you to be His Child!!!!

God knows you by name! You know other children by their names. List them, call them out daily and praise God for them.

PRAISING GOD FOR THE CHLDREN:

_____

_____

_____

_____

_____

_____

_____

_____

_____

_____

_____

_____

_____

_____

_____

_____

_____

_____

DAY 20

Cheerful Giving

II Corinthians 9:7-- Every man according as he purposeth in his heart, [so let him give]; not grudgingly, or of necessity: for God loveth a cheerful giver (KJV)

PRAISE DAY 20—Praise the Lord in your giving! Yes! You can! When you give, no matter what it is or how much it is, rejoice in the Lord, giving Him praise because He has blessed you to be a blessing to others. The Bible says in Deuteronomy 8:18 that God is the One who gives us POWER to obtain WEALTH! That's right! God empowers us to be wealthy and prosperous! When we give, a feeling of prosperity should be reflected in our attitude! If you can't give money, give of your time and/or service. There is always—and I do mean ALWAYS—someone who is worse off than you! Not only does God love a cheerful giver, but you will REAP what you SOW! Today, diligently seek and find SOMEONE who NEEDS YOU! Bless them in a way that God will be pleased with you. Then, REJOICE and be cheerful! Be blessed!

This week, purposely seek out an opportunity to bless someone! It does not matter if you think or believe that the recipient of your blessing is less off than you because you cannot tell, by looking at someone, if they are in need or not! Just be prayerful and purposeful and allow the Spirit of God to lead you! Praise God for an even greater blessing upon that person's life!

PRAISE REPORT:

_____

_____

_____

_____

_____

_____

_____

_____

_____

_____

_____

_____

_____

_____

DAY 21

Shabach God!

Psalm 63:3-- Because thy loving-kindness [is] better than life, my lips shall praise [*SHABACH*] thee. (KJV)

PRAISE DAY 21—Shabach God! The word "praise" appears in the King James Version of the Bible over 248 times in 216 verses from Genesis to Revelation! The original Hebrew and Greek texts, however, offer us several renditions of the word "praise". The translation of praise in Psalm 63:3 is "shabach" which means to celebrate in loud tone, to shout out in praise! This form of praise is the most liberating! It gives you freedom to dance and sing, shout, clap your hands and do whatever you need to do in order to "get your praise on"! This perfected type of praise is not inhibited by surroundings! It is not ashamed or stifled! Today, we have reason to rejoice and be glad! Our Savior lives! Our Lord reigns! Our King rules! He is everlasting! He is our Beginning and He is our Ending! We will rest, reign and rule with Him! Just as David says, simply because of His loving-kindness, which is GREATER THAN LIFE, my lips, my hands, and my voice will SHABACH GOD!

I saw a video on the internet where a woman was stopped at a traffic light. She got out of her car and started dancing and shouting, obviously praising God! I know that some would think she's "crazy" and others would say, "That's embarrassing". I just wished I knew what it was that gave her such joy so that I could join her in her praise! Today, just take a moment to SHABACH God! It can be on your job, at home, at church, anywhere! Just start by thanking Him and allow your spirit to elevate you to a place where you let loose of your inhibitions and just give God a shout of Praise!

Write your SHABACH praise experience below!

_____

_____

_____

_____

_____

_____

_____

_____

_____

_____

_____

_____

_____

DAY 22

God's Protection

Psalm 121:8-- The LORD shall preserve your going out and your coming in from this time forth, and even forevermore.

PRAISE DAY 22—Psalm 121 reassures us that no matter what is going on in our lives, not matter where we are, God's got our backs! There are times when you may feel as if you are running in the mud. You may feel weary, worn out, busted and disgusted. But, know this; as it has been said on numerous occasions, if God brings you to it, He will take you *through* it!

We just have to submit and surrender to whatever it is that God is trying to do in our lives. We may not understand it, but God's plan is greater that where we are right now. He sees further down the road than we can; He knows more than we know! His thoughts are not our thoughts and His ways are not our ways (Isaiah 55:8).

The question you may be asking yourself is; "What do I do while I am 'running in this mud'?" The answer is simple—Praise God for His deliverance! Follow the pattern set in Psalm 121:1 by keeping your eyes focused on the Lord. Be encouraged in knowing

---

that the Lord is our help (verse 2), the Lord will not allow us to be moved out of His will for us and He always has His eyes on us because He never sleeps(verses 3 and 4). He is our keeper, our comfort, our preservation and our protection (verses 5-8). Choose this day not to worry or be anxious! When you feel as if you are "stuck", just rehearse these verses found in Psalm 121 and praise God in the midst of your struggle!

PRAISE REPORT!

_____

_____

_____

_____

_____

_____

_____

_____

_____

_____

_____

_____

DAY 23

God's Blessing in the Valley

Psalm 23:4—Yea, though I walk through the valley of the
　　　shadow of death,
　　　I will fear no evil;
　　　For You *are* with me;
　　　Your rod and Your staff, they comfort me.

PRAISE DAY 23—The verse above is found in one of my favorite Psalms. It is the Psalm where David compares his relationship with God to that of a shepherd and his sheep. Sheep have a tendency to wander in all directions, in pursuit of greener grass. While doing so, they wander into spaces and places where they find themselves in trouble. The shepherd uses his rod and staff to bring the sheep away from trouble and back into the flock.

　　Contrary to what some may think, the shepherd's rod was not used to "beat" the sheep. If he did, the shepherd would damage the sheep's skin with cuts and bruises which decreases the sheep's value. I have observed a few county fairs where sheep were being judged and the judge would pull back the sheep's wool to look at its skin to ensure that the sheep is healthy and disease free. Among other things then, the rod was used to gently guide the sheep in the right direction. The shepherd also used the rod to fight off wild animals such as lions, and bears!

Just knowing that our Lord is willing to be a comfort to us, even when we walk into a valley situation, we can still praise Him as we realize He still loves us and we are valuable to Him! We can rejoice because even in our darkest hour, the Lord is still with us!

Identify a *dark* time in your life where you thought you were not going to make it. Write it down and include how the Lord brought you out!

PRAISE REPORT!

_____

_____

_____

_____

_____

_____

_____

_____

_____

_____

_____

_____

_____

DAY 24

God Has Given Us Dominion

Genesis 1:26--Then God said, "Let Us make man in Our image, according to Our likeness; let them have dominion over the fish of the sea, over the birds of the air, and over the cattle, over all [fn] the earth and over every creeping thing that creeps on the earth."

PRAISE DAY 24—Why do you walk around with your head hung down? Why do you fear the unknown? Why do you say things like, "the devil has really been on my back this week?" Haven't you heard? Haven't you read? God has given us dominion over everything He has created!

To have dominion means to be in supreme authority over something. Our Father was so careful during the creation process that He "saved the best for last"! He put His final touches on us when He created us and He did so with His own hands! Therefore, let us hold to our position of domination over Satan and all of his devices! Don't fear when you feel as if you are being spiritually attacked. Instead, just throw your hands up, in surrender to God, and give our Lord the praise that He so richly deserves!

What have you been struggling with? Sickness or disease? Mental issues? Depression? Distress? You may be taking medication, but even in the midst of your trial, you can give God praise! Write down those things that are troubling you and find a corresponding, correlating Scripture to combat what you are going through. Find your "praise message" in the Word of God!

MY TROUBLES	MY VICTORY SCRIPTURE

DAY 25

God, I Trust YOU

Psalm 56:11-- For In God I have put my trust;
I will not be afraid.
What can man do to me?

PRAISE DAY 25—Now that we know God has given us dominion, we have more reason to trust Him! Although we will experience trials and tribulations, nevertheless, we should continue to put and keep our trust in the Lord!

The entire 56th Number of Psalms is about handling our fears in the time of adversity. David, according to the introduction to this Psalm, wrote this poem when David found refuge with the Philistines in Gath (I Samuel 21 and I Samuel 27). David was right to challenge by saying, "What can man do to me?" He was in Gath, a town of the Philistines. If you remember David's story, he is the one who killed the Philistines' hero, Goliath (I Samuel 17:4-49). One might quickly assume that the Philistines would be enemies to David and the enemy's camp would be the last place where David would find refuge.

David understood that by putting his trust in God, he had nothing to fear! I admonish you to take the same stand! Trust God, even in the face of your enemies and give Him praise!

All of us, at one time or another have or have had people in our lives that caused us some grief. There are people who we have identified as enemies because of some wrong we believe they have committed against us. Today is the day for your deliverance! Write down the names of those persons who have hurt you and those you have been fearful of. Forgive them and walk in praise!

There is power in forgiveness!

_____

_____

_____

_____

_____

_____

_____

_____

_____

_____

_____

_____

_____

DAY 26

The Lord is Keeping Me

Psalm 139:14-- I will praise You, for I am fearfully and
wonderfully made; [fn] Marvelous are Your works,
And that my soul knows very well.

PRAISE DAY 26—The verse in this particular Psalm is very special to me. Today, at my age, I thank God daily for my life, my health and my strength. He constantly reminds me that I am as healthy as I am, because He made me, He knows all about me, He loves me and He is keeping me! People ask me all the time about how I am able to do the things that I do! I am constantly on the move, for the Lord and for myself! I try not to sit still too long.

I remember one day when I was raking my front yard of leaves, the mail man asked me how I was doing. My first response was in the form of a complaint about all of the leaves in my yard and the fact that I had to rake them by myself. To my surprise, my mailman looked at me, smiled and said, "Isn't that a blessing! You are still able to rake your own front yard!" I thought about it for a few seconds and realized what I already knew and that is he's right! It is a blessing! The Lord is keeping me!

Contributed by
Ethel D. Ellis (AKA: "Mother Ellis")

Think about those times in your life when you knew it was nobody but the Lord and the fact that He is keeping you, and you were encouraged!

PRAISING GOD Because He is Keeping Me:

_____

_____

_____

_____

_____

_____

_____

_____

_____

_____

_____

_____

_____

_____

_____

_____

_____

_____

DAY 27

God is My Strength

Psalm 46:1-- To the Chief Musician. A Psalm of the sons of Korah. A Song for Alamoth. God is our refuge and strength, A very present help in trouble.

PRAISE DAY 27—Let's face it! We all have troubles; some of us more than others. And, there are times when we have been distressed, stressed, anxious, perplexed, confused, frustrated and more.

We have to remember that the Lord has never promised us that we would not have troubles! Quite the contrary, He says in Job 14:1, "Man who is born of woman is of few days and full of trouble." Even though God has never promised us a rose garden, He has promised that He would never leave us nor would He forsake us (Hebrews 13:5b).

Our problem is that we try to handle our problems and carry our burdens ourselves. So, today, right now, just begin to speak those things that have been a burden to you, lift up your hands towards heaven and turn them over to Jesus! He can and He will work it out! Give God praise for your peace and joy because He is your strength!

PRAISING GOD FOR HIS STRENGTH:

DAY 28

I Am Healed!

Isaiah 53:5— But He *was* wounded for our transgressions,
   He was bruised for our iniquities;
   The chastisement for our peace *was* upon Him,
   And by His stripes we are healed.

PRAISE DAY 28—Sickness and disease; it is all around us! You may be the ill one or you may know someone close to you who may be sick and in need of healing. The Scripture above gives us hope in the healing nature of our Lord! He is still a healer and we have to believe that! Sometimes, we have to be like blind Bartimaeus. His story is found in Mark 10:46-52. He was healed by Jesus after he cried out, stood up, and made his way to Him, pushing and shoving his way to his healing!

There are times when you too have to ignore the crowd, or the words of your friends and family. You have to rise up out of your circumstances and cry out in a loud voice to the on One who can make a difference in your situation. You know what kind of healing you need—physical, emotional, mental, spiritual, etc.—and Christ is the only One who has suffered, bled and died so that you might have a more abundant life, here on earth as well as eternal life with Him in heaven! Rejoice now, and be glad, for the Lord is Jehovah-Rapha, the God Who Healed!

Rejoice for today is the day of your healing! Believe that God can and He will whether in this life or the next! Trust Him to perform His Word!

LIST: Where/who needs healing in your life today?

1. _____

2. _____

3. _____

4. _____

5. _____

6. _____

7. _____

8. _____

9. _____

10. _____

11. _____

12. _____

DAY 29

Praise His Kindness Towards Us

Psalm 117:2-- For His merciful kindness is great toward us,
And the truth of the LORD *endures* forever.
Praise the LORD!

PRAISE DAY 29—When was the last time you were kind to someone? Kindness can be in the form of thanking someone for something they have done for you. It can be as simple as allowing someone to go in line, in front of you. Kindness can be preparing a meal for someone, paying for someone's gas at the gas station, hugging a child or even patting someone on the back for a job well done.

Think about the last time someone was kind to you and how it made you feel; especially if you felt you were unworthy of their kindness.

God's kindness towards us is not based upon our "righteousness" because we are not righteous enough to deserve His kindness. As it is indicated in the verse above, His kindness towards us is merciful and extended to us regardless of our short comings! Come on, now! Praise Him!

Now that you know that the Lord has extended His grace towards you, you extend kindness, merciful kindness that is, towards someone else! Seek out an opportunity TODAY to be kind!

PRAISE REPORT:

_____

_____

_____

_____

_____

_____

_____

_____

_____

_____

_____

_____

_____

_____

_____

_____

DAY 30

Praise God Continually

Psalm 34:1 -- *A Psalm* of David when he pretended madness before Abimelech, who drove him away, and he departed.

I will bless the LORD at all times;
His praise *shall* continually *be* in my mouth.

PRAISE DAY 30—Did you see the introduction to this Psalm? It indicates to us the David was in fear of his life when he was in the presence of Abimelech (Achish) while he was in Gath (I Samuel 21:10-15). He pretended to be demented in order to keep from being harmed. After his deliverance, he penned this Psalm.

This serves as a reminder to us to praise God even in our trials and tests. No, we are not encouraged to pretend to be insane to get out of trouble; but we are encouraged to praise the Lord our God constantly. We should praise Him when our bank accounts are full and when they are empty. We should praise Him when all is well with us and even when all hell is breaking loose! What have you got to lose by giving God the praise that He so richly deserves? Doesn't He know about your struggles? Doesn't He know your pain and your discomforts? He knows and He cares!

Identify a situation where you wanted to cry, now praise God for bringing you out of that situation! When you encounter a negative situation today, even if it is something as simple as a "traffic jam", instead of griping or groaning, start praising the Lord!

PRAISING GOD CONTINUALLY:

_____

_____

_____

_____

_____

_____

_____

_____

_____

_____

_____

_____

_____

_____

DAY 31

God Gives Me Rest

Psalm 23:2a—He makes me to lie down in green pastures;

PRAISE DAY 31—Every once in a while, everybody and *every body* needs to rest! The first part of verse 2 in the 23rd Psalm, says that the Lord <u>makes</u> me lie down in green pastures! I don't know about you, but there have been times in my life where life was wearing me out! Stress on the job, stress at home because of the stress on the job. Finances were out of control. Things were just not going well! Little did I realize at the time was that the biggest thing I was in need of was rest!

Sometimes, when we are stressed out and discombobulated, and we are feeling the pressures of life all around us, what we really need during those times is rest! Give your body, your mind and your life a rest! Spend some quiet praise and worship time with the Lord! Take some time with your family, go to a park, go to the beach, go camping; or sit in solitude, just anything that will take your mind away from what is pressuring you!

While you are doing so, give God a PRAISE!

Plan your REST day of Praise:

_____

_____

_____

_____

_____

_____

_____

_____

_____

_____

_____

_____

_____

_____

_____

_____

_____

DAY 32

I'm in Him & He's in Me

John 15:5—"I am the vine, you *are* the branches. He who abides in Me, and I in him, bears much fruit; for without Me you can do nothing.

PRAISE DAY 32—This verse reminds me that I am one with Christ when I accept Him as my Lord and Savior! That means, everywhere I am, everywhere that I might be, everything I feel, everything I hope is also in Him! Christ knows all about every struggle and every triumph!

Just like a seed, everything that I need to reach my full potential in Christ, is already in me! Anything additional that I may have need of, He will provide. *Everything* I am and hope to be are in Christ Jesus. In order for me to reach my full potential, I must remain in Him. Be encouraged today and be reminded that if we abide in Christ, He abides in us! When we are one with Him, there is nothing that we will not be able to achieve or accomplish (John 15:7).

Rejoice and be happy because you are one with Christ!

Take a few minutes and write down your gifts and talents. Then, identify how, where and when you can use these in order to glorify Christ!

PRAISE GOD FOR YOUR TALENTS AND GIFTS HE'S PLACED IN YOU!

_____

_____

_____

_____

_____

_____

_____

_____

_____

_____

_____

_____

_____

_____

_____

_____

_____

DAY 33

I Have Abundant Life in Christ

John 10:10-- "The thief does not come except to steal, and to kill, and to destroy. I have come that they may have life, and that they may have *it* more abundantly.

PRAISE DAY 33—When things are not going right in our lives, it becomes easy to shut down. For a lot of us, when we shut down, the first thing we have a tendency to let go of is our prayer life and our participation in church activities. What we must realize is that it is not God who has caused this misery in our lives!

The real enemy is the same one who has been harassing the body of Christ for generations! That is, Satan! He comes to steal our joy, kill our relationships, and destroy our lives! But know this; he can only do what God allows! And, if the Lord allows it, it means we are stronger, through Christ Jesus, as a result of the matter! We have to realize that God is only working things out for our good and our betterment. He has promised us abundant life! So even though I may be going through something, I can be assured that God is working it out for my good and He is directing my path towards a more abundant life in Christ Jesus! Let us rejoice and be glad!

Take a moment and thank God for all that He has brought you through and thank Him for everything He is bringing you TO!

PRAISE REPORT:

_____

_____

_____

_____

_____

_____

_____

_____

_____

_____

_____

_____

_____

_____

_____

_____

_____

_____

DAY 34

Delivering Power of Praise

Psalm 150:6-- Let everything that has breath praise the
LORD. Praise the LORD!

PRAISE **DAY 34**—We have all heard the saying, "looks can be deceiving"; and I can testify to the validity of that statement. Several years ago I walked around with a smile on my face and displayed a pleasant attitude as I interacted with my family, co-workers and people in general. My outward appearance depicted that of a happy, contented woman who had it all together. NOT SO! On the inside I was filled with sorrow and a deep sadness.

For a period of about two years I was under attack by a spirit of depression. I say that it was a spirit because I really had no real reason to be sad all the time. I was saved and delivered from a life of sin, I had a good job, finances were not a problem, I had loving family members, and good friends to spend time with. Yet, every morning I woke up so depressed, that it took every ounce of my strength just to get up out of bed. Every night, I buried my face in my pillow and cried myself to sleep.

One Sunday during the devotional period of the morning services a deacon read Psalm 150, and something clicked in my spirit. I went home and read that passage of Scripture over and over again, and realized that it was instructing me to praise the Lord everywhere—in the sanctuary, in the firmament. Praise the Lord for who He is and for what He has done. Praise Him with all kinds of musical instruments. Verse six of Psalm 150 says, "let everything that has breath praise the Lord." As I read those words, deliverance began to take place. I realized that I did not have a trumpet or a loud sounding cymbal. I was too sad to even dance. But I did have breath. So every morning from then on when I woke up, with my first breath I would simply say "Praise the Lord". Every night before I fell asleep the last words I breathed out was, "Praise the Lord." It wasn't very long afterwards that I became aware that I was not sad any more. The spirit of depression had been replaced with a spirit of praise.

Because I have breath, I will continue to bless the name of the Lord, rejoice and be glad and give Him praise.

Contributed by
Dr. Brenda Mullin
Sisters In Support Ministries

There is power in praise! Write your praise report below!

_____

_____

_____

_____

_____

_____

_____

_____

_____

_____

_____

_____

_____

_____

_____

_____

_____

_____

DAY 35
Simply Because He is God

Psalm 18:31 -- For who *is* God, except the LORD?
And who *is* a rock, except our God?

PRAISE DAY 35—Who is greater than our God? Who is mightier? Who can do the things that our God can do? There are so many stories in the Bible that encourage us to have faith in God! There are so many prophecies that we would be foolish not to believe that Jesus Christ is the Son of God, and accept Him as our Lord and savior!

How can we deny the One who created us and the world around us? You can simply review the Book of Genesis and the story of creation to realize how wonderfully powerful our God is! He created the light in the middle of darkness! He made the earth, the trees, the creatures of the sea and the ones on the land. He made plants and trees to bear fruit. He made the sun, the moon and the stars. And after He had everything prepared, He made man!

How excellent He is! He knew that man would need the sun to warm him in the day time and the moon at night to remind him to rest. Man would need the water to drink and he would need the fruit from the trees to feed himself. And, he would need the animals to keep him company! God is God and He is Awesome!

Pick up your Bible and read your favorite Bible story where God presented Himself, strong and mighty! Realize that what He did then, He can still do today! Summarize your Bible story below.

PRAISE GOD for He is GOD:

_____

_____

_____

_____

_____

_____

_____

_____

_____

_____

_____

_____

_____

_____

_____

_____

_____

_____

DAY 36

Seven Times a Day

Psalm 119:164-- Seven times a day I praise You,
Because of Your righteous judgments.

PRAISE DAY 36—Have you ever stopped long enough during your day to just Praise God? Some of you may be asking yourself, "How can I praise God seven times a day?" Or, you may be saying to yourself, "I can't think of seven things to praise God for, on a daily basis!"

When I think of His goodness and all that He has done for me, I can't help but to thank Him and praise Him! This praise day is simple. Write down at least seven things that you are thankful for and give God praise! Praise Him daily as you increase your list!

Here are a few examples:

1. He is a Righteous Judge—when I should have been cast out, God stepped in and delivered me.
2. He woke me up this morning. I was in my right mind.
3. He put joy in my heart
4. He loves me unconditionally
5. My household is blessed
6. He is my strength
7. He is my fortress

Now, you start your own list!

PRAISING GOD SEVEN TIMES A DAY:

_____

_____

_____

_____

_____

_____

_____

_____

_____

_____

_____

_____

_____

_____

_____

_____

_____

_____

_____

DAY 37

He Wipes My Tears Away

Revelation 21:4-- "And God will wipe away every tear from their eyes; there shall be no more death, nor sorrow, nor crying. There shall be no more pain, for the former things have passed away."

PRAISE DAY 37—Let's face it! Life has a way of bringing us to tears! We have financial trouble, we have family problems, and we have sickness and diseases. There is famine in the land. We get emotionally distressed by all of the wickedness that goes on in the world. There is killing, death and destruction all around us.

Additionally, there are senseless, random shootings and killings, the murders of innocent people. There are plane crashes with numerous lives being destroyed. We see prejudices and injustices that bring us to tears. And, there are countless other incidents that cause our hearts to ache.

As humans and even more, as Christians, we cannot sit by and watch these things happen without them touching us and bringing us to the point of moaning. We have to understand that Jesus was filled with the same compassion when he saw a crowd of people who did not have faith enough to believe (John 11:35).

Our greatest burden should be when we see lost souls.

Nevertheless, our hope remains in Christ Jesus! We can rejoice!

Today, when you see and/or experience a tragedy, pray for everyone involved. Write it down and pray for the souls of those involved. Pray that the Lord will allow them the opportunity to be saved! Then, praise Him for their deliverance and salvation.

Praise in the midst of tragedy:

_____

_____

_____

_____

_____

_____

_____

_____

_____

_____

_____

_____

_____

_____

_____

DAY 38

He is My Righteous Judge

II Timothy 4:8-- Finally, there is laid up for me the crown of righteousness, which the Lord, the righteous Judge, will give to me on that Day, and not to me only but also to all who have loved His appearing.

PRAISE DAY 38—Have you ever been falsely accused of something? How did you feel? What happened when you tried to defend yourself? Were you able to convince your accuser of your innocence? Did you try? How did that work out for you? Did you feel better or worse? How long ago was the accusation? How do you feel about it today?

At some point in life, I believe that we all have been accused of something that we did not do. The closer in relationship the accuser is, the harder it is for us to accept the accusation without trying to convince our loved one of the "truth".

An incident that comes to my mind is when one of my family members called me and made loud, boisterous accusations towards me. The accusations were covered in profanities and obscenities. Before I could offer any rebuttal, the person on the other end of the line hung up! Needless to say, I was dumbfounded, devastated and hurt!

With my eyes full of tears, I heard the Spirit of the Lord say to me, "Call back and apologize."

Again, I was confused! I said, "Apologize?? Me?? I didn't do anything!"

The Spirit of the Lord said to me, "There must have been something you did in order for the accusation to come forth."

I called and apologized to my accuser. My accuser quickly said, "Thank you," and hung up again. Although that was not the response I was looking for, before I could feel bad again, I realized that the apology was not for my accuser, but it was for me! I was free in knowing that I did what God would want me to do!

One thing is for sure, God sees and He cares! He knows the truth, the whole truth and every aspect of the truth! He will not hold us responsible for what others do to us, but He will hold us responsible for what we do to others! He is our Righteous Judge and it is in His eyes that I want to be found blameless! So, go ahead! Apologize! For the Lord is our Righteous Judge! Praise Him for our heavenly reward that awaits us in His presence!

Make a list of people you have been holding a grudge against and/or those who you need to apologize to. Let the Spirit of the Lord lead you! After you have done what you need to do, take a few moments and thank the Lord for allowing you the opportunity to get it right while you yet live! Forgiveness is liberating!

PRAISING GOD FOR HIS RIGHTEOUS JUDGEMENTS:

_____

_____

_____

_____

_____

_____

_____

_____

_____

_____

_____

_____

_____

_____

_____

_____

DAY 39

He Touched Me

Mark 10:13a-- **Then they brought little children to Him, that He might touch them;**

PRAISE DAY 39—One day, I found myself in despair. There was something personal going on in my life that I could not tell anyone else but God. This situation was so devastating (so I thought) that the mere thought of it would bring me to tears and audible cries. Then, as I was crying out to the Lord, the Holy Spirit brought this verse above to my remembrance.

I said, "Yes, Lord! I need a touch! I need a hug! I need to feel Your presence!"

Then the Spirit of the Lord said to me, "Reach up and let go!" I lifted my head from the floor, with my eyes full of tears, I stretched my arms towards heaven, pretty much like a child reaching up to parents in order to be picked up.

Then, suddenly, like fresh rain, I felt the Spirt of the Lord *fall* on me! Immediately my joy was restored and my stress was replaced with sweet rest!

Sometimes, we have to surrender our burdens to the Lord, and rest in Him! He wants to touch us with His presence. Let go and let Him touch you!

Put on your worship music and bow down before the Lord God. Pray and ask Jesus to TOUCH you! If you have time and if you are willing, stay there until you *feel* His touch! Then, praise Him for touching you! Write your praise report below.

HE TOUCHED ME:

_____

_____

_____

_____

_____

_____

_____

_____

_____

_____

_____

_____

_____

_____

_____

_____

_____

DAY 40

The Lord Reigns

Psalm 93:1 -- The LORD reigns, He is clothed with majesty;
The LORD is clothed,
He has girded Himself with strength.
Surely the world is established, so that it cannot be moved

PRAISE DAY 40—No matter what happens to you today, no matter what you are going through right now, remember that the Lord REIGNS! He rules! He is supreme! There is none like Him! He is all powerful! He is Almighty! He is the Righteous One, the Omnipotent, Omnipresent and Omniscient One! There is none like Him in all of heaven and earth!

So, as Psalm 43:5 reads;

Why are you cast down, O my soul?

And why are you disquieted within me?

Hope in God;

For I shall yet praise Him,

The help of my countenance and my God.

In other words, I don't have to worry, I don't have to be afraid and I don't have to walk around with my head hung down!

My victory is at hand because it is in the hands of my Lord and Savior, Jesus Christ! With Him, we WIN!

Who do you say that the Lord God is? Who is He to you? Praise Him because He is good and He is GOD!

GIVE GOD PRAISE:

_____

_____

_____

_____

_____

_____

_____

_____

_____

_____

_____

_____

_____

_____

DAY 41

I Can Come Before Him

Hebrews 4:16—Let us therefore come boldly to the throne of grace, that we may obtain mercy and find grace to help in time of need.

PRAISE **DAY 41**—There is nothing hidden from God. There is nowhere we can go and He is not already there. There is no sin we can commit that He does not already know about! Neither is that anything that we could do that would cause Him to love us any less.

Throughout my career with a state prison system, I have had several positions where I had to conduct extensive interviews with offenders. Many times, they would be reluctant to answer my questions because the questions as well as the answers would be embarrassing! I found that when I would let them know that every question I ask I already had the answer and that I just needed them to agree with what was in their record, more often than not, they would sit back in the chair, relax and boldly respond to my questions. Several of them have said to me, "Since you already know, I might as well tell you!"

Since the Lord already knows, we might as well tell Him and agree with our record! So, let's just confess and get it over with!

Afterwards, we can rejoice because our burden—the dead weight of guilt—has been lifted!

Identify something you have kept to yourself for years that you now need to confess! Then rejoice because you have been forgiven!

PRAISING GOD FOR HIS FORGIVENESS:

_____

_____

_____

_____

_____

_____

_____

_____

_____

_____

_____

_____

_____

_____

_____

_____

_____

DAY 42

The Lord Keeps My Mind

Isaiah 26:3—You will keep him in perfect peace,
Whose mind is stayed on You,
Because he trusts in You.

PRAISE DAY 42—Where does confusion begin? Where does doubt begin? Where do distrust, unfaithfulness, arguments and dissention? All of these begin in the mind. Our minds are constantly moving information, real or imagined, through our brains. The only times it stops (we hope) is when we fall into deep, deep sleeps.

This verse in Isaiah's book tells us how we can get and keep garbage out of our minds. If we keep and focus our minds on the Lord and all of His goodness, He will keep us in perfect peace! When I wake up in the mornings, the first words out of my mouth are "Thank You, Jesus!"

Wake up with the Lord on your mind! He will keep you in a peaceful state of mind with praise on your lips. If you want to be blessed, that is: set apart, favored, protected, comforted, lifted, covered and more—then put the Lord first in all that you do! Allow Him to be the focus in your mind. Allow Him to lead, guide and direct you.

What do you need to surrender to the Lord today? Write it/them down and trust Him. Whenever those things try to creep up in your mind to distract you from Him, sing a song of praise! With God at the head of your journey, you can praise Him with assurance of peace!

PRAISING GOD FOR KEEPING YOUR MIND:

_____

_____

_____

_____

_____

_____

_____

_____

_____

_____

_____

_____

_____

_____

_____

_____

DAY 43

God Causes Me to Prosper

Deuteronomy 8:18-- "And you shall remember the LORD your God, for *it is* He who gives you power to get wealth, that He may establish His covenant which He swore to your fathers, as *it is* this day.

PRAISE DAY 43—Read this verse and read it again! Did you see it? Or, did you miss it? The Lord our God gives us power to obtain wealth! He has filled us with skills, gifts and talents. He will bless us with His knowledge! It is His will for us to prosper so that His covenant, His promises, can be fulfilled. All He wants is for us to remember and recognize that He is our Lord!

Growing up, my mother would always make sure that when we went out, we were dressed in our best. She did so because she recognized that people would look at us and would either blame her or congratulate her on our appearance. She always said she didn't want us to look as if we didn't belong to her! Wow!

If my mother wanted to make sure that we looked like we belonged to her, how much more do you think and believe that God wants us to look like we belong to Him! Give God some praise because we are His!

The Lord has put gifts and talents in us that He wants to use for His glory and your prosperity. Make a list of those gifts and talents that you have. How can you use them to bless God? How can you use them to prosper? You might have different gifts and talents that you can use for different reasons. For example; your gift to sing can be used in church. Your talent to sew might be used to prosper you!

PRAISING GOD FOR His gifts and talents in you:

_____

_____

_____

_____

_____

_____

_____

_____

_____

_____

_____

_____

_____

_____

DAY 44

Be Still--He's God

Psalm 46:10--Be still, and know that I *am* God;
I will be exalted among the nations,
I will be exalted in the earth!

PRAISE DAY 44—Devastation all around us! Needless killings, abuse, mistreatment, wars and rumors of wars! These things and more are happening every day. More and more, we find it difficult to watch the news. There is so much negativity in the world that one might be encouraged to ask, "Where is God?"

The verse in Psalm 46 reminds us that no matter what we see or what happens in the world, God is still in control! There is nothing that happens without His permission. We can hold fast to His promise that His Word will be fulfilled. We can be assured that He does not change! He is everlasting, the First and the Last, the Beginning and the End! He is exalted among the nations and He is exalted in the earth! Therefore, while we have breath, let us Praise the LORD (Psalm 150)!

Praise the Lord because He is still in control! Write your concerns about today's issues and turn them over the God. Write your praise report below.

_____

_____

_____

_____

_____

_____

_____

_____

_____

_____

_____

_____

_____

_____

_____

_____

_____

DAY 45

It's Not My Fight, Anyway

Psalm 24:8-- **For Who *is* this King of glory?
The LORD strong and mighty,
The LORD mighty in battle.**

PRAISE DAY 45—I remember a time when my youngest sister was about 7 years of age. She was playing in a sandbox at the park when a boy who was older and larger than her, came to the sandbox and began bullying her, trying to force her to leave the box.

Although my sister was not relinquishing her position in the box, I could still hear fear in her voice as she was resisting his demands. The boy began making threats and started saying he was going to hit my sister.

About this time, I arrived at the sand box. Being older and larger than the bully, I was confident as I approached the sandbox and in defense of my sister, asked the question, "What's going on here? Are you bothering my sister?"

Before the boy could answer, my sister looked up and saw that I was standing behind her. She quickly stood up, grabbed my hand and with newfound courage, shouted at the boy, "Go ahead! You wanna hit me? Hit me then!" She knew that I was there to defend her from any attack!

God is our refuge, our strong tower and He is mighty in battle! Just like my sister, there are many battles that we face that we don't have to fight ourselves! We only have to realize that the Lord will fight the battle for us, if only we realize He is standing there with us! From enemies on the job, to enemies in schools, God is still the strongest one! You hold your peace and allow the Lord to fight your battle!

Give the Lord your battle today!

DAY 46

I Can Let Go; Let God

I Peter 5:6, 7—Therefore humble yourselves under the mighty hand of God, that He may exalt you in due time, 7) casting all your care upon Him, for He cares for you.

PRAISE DAY 46—What's on your mind right now? Concerns about your finances? Concerns about your children? Concerns about sickness—either yours or someone close to you? Are you concerned about your future? Well, is there anything you can do right now about either of your concerns? If you can't, then your only recourse is to let it go!

When we humble ourselves before God, we realize that our situation is much larger than us and we have to say, "I can't do this! Lord, You take over!"

Too many times, we find ourselves in situations where we struggle, trying to "fix it", only to make things worse. We have to humble ourselves because we think our intellect is such that we are smart enough to solve all of our own problems! Well, when you get tired, when you get sick and tired, you know it is time—actually past time—for you to let it go!

List those things and people that you have been holding on to, for far too long. Pray over them one more time and before you get off your knees, release them into the mighty hands of God! He can do more with these issues than you can. Rejoice for the Lord has lifted your heavy heart!

PRAISING GOD FOR HIS STRENGTH:

_____

_____

_____

_____

_____

_____

_____

_____

_____

_____

_____

_____

_____

_____

_____

_____

_____

DAY 47

God's Angels

Hebrews 13:2—Do not neglect to show hospitality to strangers, for by this some have entertained angels without knowing it. (NIV)

PRAISE DAY 47—Although, the above Scripture is not from Psalms, it is the Bible verse that speaks to my heart of my love for the Lord and makes me sing His praises. I've heard it said but I don't know who said it that "when God can't be there He sends His angels. When His angels can't be there God sends us."

How many times have we met a stranger and told them they were an angel to us because of something they did for us?

I do believe in miracles that are the direct result of an angelic intervention but I also believe that God places people in our lives for miraculous (and some not so miraculous) reasons so that they can be there in person to help us out when a need arises. Those people may not know it themselves at the time but God has a way of using us to serve His needs.

There are times in many of our lives in which we have found ourselves or our loved ones in the middle of a life-changing crisis or even facing danger when someone we may not know happens to step in to provide assistance or even save us from harm or possibly even death.

The timing of their appearance may or may not seem as miraculous as a scene from a Hollywood blockbuster but we know in our hearts that the Lord had a guiding hand in how the event played out. Some of us can't help but breakdown and cry while others will jump around with joy singing out praises to the Lord. Regardless of the outcome, we still praise Him knowing that the event could have gone in a different direction.

When we give praise to the Lord for all the times He's stepped in to be with us in our time of need or sent someone to be there in His place, we should also ask the Lord to humbly use us for His benefit in the same way. When we do something for the benefit of others in God's name, we should do it in secret as stated in Matthew 6:1-4.

As Mother Teresa said, "Some people come into our life as blessings. Some people come into our life as lessons." Matthew 12:50. Jesus said, "For whoever does the will of My Father who is in heaven, he is My brother and sister and mother." Let us pray that we always do the Lord's will and be a blessing to everyone we encounter in this world and we will be rewarded in heaven.

Contributed by
Janet Sebring

Seek out an opportunity to be an "angel" for someone today! Pray and ask the Lord to guide you and use you today! There are many opportunities to be used by Him; we just have to be sensitive enough to hear His voice and understand His instructions. Share your testimony below.

PRAISE HIM BECAUSE HE USES US:

_____

_____

_____

_____

_____

_____

_____

_____

_____

_____

_____

_____

_____

_____

_____

_____

DAY 48

For the Things I Can't See

II Kings 6:17—And Elisha prayed, and said, Lord, I pray thee, open his eyes, that he may see. And the Lord opened the eyes of the young man; and he saw: and, behold, the mountain was full of horses and chariots of fire round about Elisha.

PRAISE DAY 48—One snowy morning, my family and I were on our way to visit my mother, who lived about two and a half hours drive away from us. Shortly after we left home and started down the highway, my oldest daughter who was about 8 years of age at the time, shouted for us to stop. Hearing the distress in her voice, my husband pulled our van off to the side of the road. We both turned to look at her and asked what the matter was.

Very matter-of-factly, she replied, "We forgot to pray!" Sure enough, this was one time when we left our driveway, on our way out of town, and we did not pray before we left. In obedience to God and as a result of her outburst, we all bowed our heads as we allowed our daughter to lead us in prayer.

The prayer only lasted a few moments. However, a few moments up the road, we saw a vehicle that had swerved into our lane, due to the snow and ice on the road. It had crossed the road into what would have been our lane and ended in a ditch. People who were driving behind the vehicle were getting out of their cars and rushing to the rescue. We quickly realized, had we not stopped for that brief moment of prayer, that car would have crashed into us! We all rejoiced as we realized that even when we can't see it, God's army is all around us and His hand continuously protects us.

Take time today to praise God for a time in your life where you know it was He who delivered you from an unseen danger!

PRAISING GOD FOR HIS PROTECTION:

_____

_____

_____

_____

_____

_____

_____

_____

_____

_____

_____

_____

DAY 49

God My Miracle Maker

Psalm 111:4—And He has made His wonderful works to be remembered; The LORD is gracious and full of compassion.

PRAISE DAY 49—One day, I was out for my morning jog. Although it was spring, according to the calendar, there was still ice on the ground and trees were covered in a sheet of ice. It was the end of a bitter cold winter, as far as we Southeast Texans are concerned.

As I was jogging and talking to the Lord, I found myself voicing my concerns about the lingering cold. I was not fearful, just concerned. I was so ready for the winter to be over.

Just as I was about to allow my concerns to overwhelm me, I heard a still small voice say, "Look closer!"

I stopped in my tracks and began searching the area for whatever it was that I was supposed to being looking at more closely. All I saw was dead, lifeless, leafless trees. So, I took steps closer to one of the trees. There on the branch, encased in the ice, were several small buds of leaves! This small reminder encouraged me! God is still in control and He is still a wonderful miracle worker! We sometimes have to look for Him in the *small* things!

Take time today to seek the Lord in the small things! Listen for His voice in your quiet moments. He is all around us and there is always evidence of His presence.

PRAISING GOD FOR HIS WONDERFUL WORKS:

_____

_____

_____

_____

_____

_____

_____

_____

_____

_____

_____

_____

_____

_____

_____

_____

_____

DAY 50

God Heard My Cries

Psalm 40:1 -- [[To the chief Musician, A Psalm of David.]] I waited patiently for the LORD; and he inclined unto me, and heard my cry.

PRAISE DAY 50—There will be times in your life where all you want to do is cry! There is no problem with crying; you just have to cry to the right One! No matter what the problem is, our God can solve them! He hears our cries and He knows our struggles. He sees us in our suffering. And, because I know that He cares for me, I can still praise Him as I endure my pain.

PRAISING GOD FOR HIS STRENGTH:

_____

_____

_____

_____

_____

_____

_____

_____

_____

_____

DAY 51

There is Nothing Too Hard for God

Jeremiah 32:27--"Behold, I *am* the LORD, the God of all flesh. Is there anything too hard for Me?

PRAISE DAY 51—Jeremiah is the epitome of a suffering servant. In reading his story in his book, you will find that the major theme of his prophecies was dealing with the destruction of Jerusalem and the capture of Israel. While Jeremiah was hard pressed to deliver God's Word to the people, in their continued defiance Jeremiah suffered shame and resentment.

And as the Lord was telling Jeremiah of Israel's impending doom, He gives instructions to Jeremiah to purchase land (Jeremiah 32:26) with the promise that the land would be given back to Israel. God let Jeremiah know that although the times of destruction must be endured, it was only for the good of the people of Israel.

There are times when we go through things, times, situations and circumstances and we are confused as to why these things are happening. Rather than looking at them as a time of your failure, pray that God will open your eyes so that you can see what He is working out on your behalf! He may be decreasing you in one area of your life so that He can increase you in another!

If you are going through something right now, write it

---

down and begin praising God for what He is doing and working out in your life!

PRAISING GOD THROUGH STRUGGLES:

_____

_____

_____

_____

_____

_____

_____

_____

_____

_____

_____

_____

_____

_____

_____

_____

_____

_____

_____

DAY 52

God Knows About My Tomorrow

Matthew 6:34--"Therefore do not worry about tomorrow, for tomorrow will worry about its own things. Sufficient for the day *is* its own trouble.

PRAISE DAY 52—As a follow up on yesterday's praise, this Scripture is also provided to encourage you through your struggles and those things that you may not understand right now. The verses of Scripture in the sixth chapter of Matthew's gospel point out, God is concerned about the smallest things such as the birds of the air, fish in the sea and the grass in the fields. If He is so concerned about those things, then know He is concerned about you!

"Then why is there so much devastation in the world?" I hear you asking. Because these things must take place (Revelation 4:1) before our Lord and Savior Jesus Christ returns in the fullness of His glory!

As a word of comfort, I offer you the words of this hymn by Ira F. Stanphill, entitled "I Know Who Holds Tomorrow".

> **I don't know about tomorrow**
> **I just live from day to day**
> **I don't borrow from its sunshine**

For its skies may turn to gray

I don't worry o'er the future

For I know what Jesus said

And today I'll walk beside Him

For He knows what is ahead

Chorus:

Many things about tomorrow

I don't seem to understand

But I know who holds tomorrow

And I know who holds my hand

Search the web for your favorite rendition of this hymn and allow it to minister to you as you praise the Lord through your tomorrow! The things that we go through today will not last forever! Sing a song of praise as you thank the Lord for the new day tomorrow!

PRAISING GOD FOR TOMORROW:

_____

_____

_____

_____

_____

_____

_____

DAY 53

A Right Now Praise

I Chronicles 29:13, 14--Now therefore, our God, we thank thee, and praise thy glorious name. 14) But who am I, and what is my people, that we should be able to offer so willingly after this sort? for all things come of thee, and of thine own have we given thee. (KJV)

PRAISE DAY 53—Stop, look and listen! Look around you and see all of the things that God has blessed you with! Don't look at what you don't have, what you haven't done, or where you haven't been! As the saying goes, don't look at your life as being half empty, but look at it as being half full! As long as there is breath in your body, there is more for you to do and more for the Lord to do through you! He is not finished with you yet!

The preceding verse 12 for the above Scripture reads:

"Both riches and honor *come* from You,

And You reign over all. In Your hand *is*

power and might; In Your hand *it is* to make

great And to give strength to all."

When we understand that all things come from the Lord God, things such as power, might, greatness and wealth, we can't help but to praise Him! He reigns and He rules! Anything that we can offer to God is His already, as verse 14 points out! So, let's surrender a praise to our God!

Take a self-inventory today and thank God, praise God for all that you are and all that you have because it all comes from Him!

What are you thankful for?

_____

_____

_____

_____

_____

_____

_____

_____

_____

_____

_____

_____

_____

_____

_____

DAY 54

My Fourth Man in the Fire

Daniel 3:25--"Look!" he answered, "I see four men loose, walking in the midst of the fire; and they are not hurt, and the form of the fourth is like the Son of God."

PRAISE DAY 54—Many of us are familiar with the Biblical story of the three Hebrew boys, Shadrach, Meshach, and Abed-Nego, and how when they refused to bow down and worship King Nebuchadnezzar, God delivered them from death. They chose to stand for what is right rather than kneel before and surrender to the wrong thing (Read Daniel chapter 35).

At the king's command, they were thrown into a fiery furnace when they refused to bow down. The furnace was heated "exceedingly hot", so much so that the men who were preparing the fire were burned (Daniel 3:22). When the king was sure that the men had been consumed by the fire, he took a look into the furnace and saw that instead of three men in the flames, there were four! And, as he exclaimed, "the fourth is like the Son of God." Not only were they delivered from the fire, but even their clothes didn't smell of smoke or fire (Daniel 3:27).

Still, even in today's times, we as Christians will have to stand up for what is right in the eyes of the Lord! We will be challenged and we will be chastised for our beliefs. Our assurance lies in the truth of God's

---

Word! He will never leave us nor forsake us (Hebrews 13:5).

Know that God is with us even when we are faced with the fire of societal rejection of our Christian values and principles! We cannot, we must not bow down to the world's standard, but we must uphold the standards that God has set! Identify a lawful promotion of an act or circumstance that the world upholds and identify the Word of God, in Scripture, where the Lord rejects that practice. Write your affirmations and remember that God will be your Fourth Man in the Fire with you!

_____

_____

_____

_____

_____

_____

_____

_____

_____

_____

_____

_____

_____

_____

_____

_____

_____

DAY 55

Redeem the Time

Ephesians 5:15, 16 --See then that you walk circumspectly, not as fools but as wise, 16) redeeming the time, because the days are evil.

PRAISE DAY 18—Redeem the time, in this particular verse, means taking advantage of every opportunity to spread the Word of God, sharing the Gospel of Jesus Christ, and taking advantage of every opportunity to do good and not evil! More than ever, now is the time for us as Christians to redeem the time! We have to stop saying and thinking to ourselves that someone else is going to do the job of sharing the Gospel of Jesus. God has chosen each of us to perform this task.

When we think about sharing the Good News, we think that we have to "preach". That is not the case! There are so many ways to share the Word of God without forcing people to read the Bible, something that many of us are lacking anyway! We are afraid to talk about something that we are unsure of ourselves.

The good news about sharing God's Words is that there are ways to do it without opening your Bible! This is not only helpful for you, but also for the unchurched person you might want to witness to. You can give them a faith based greeting card that has

Scripture on it. You can write them an encouraging note. You can share with them a video from either your pastor or from another minister of the Gospel who has provided you with a Word that ministered to you. You can give them a recording of your favorite Christian music. And, you can use social media to post inspirational thoughts instead of the many, many inappropriate posts I see (and delete) on a daily basis.

Share a book with them—one that you have read—that gives them information about the Lord. Use one that you have read because the person may come back to you with questions. It would be embarrassing to say the least, if you are asked a question and your only response is, "Oh, I didn't read it!"

Find someone to share the Word of God with today!

As you praise God today, pray and ask Him to guide you as you prepare ways to share the Gospel using today's methods. Make a list of the ways and make a list of the people! May God's blessings be upon you in this endeavor!

_____

_____

_____

_____

_____

_____

_____

_____

_____

_____

_____

_____

_____

_____

_____

_____

_____

DAY 56

Praise God with My Being

Psalm 146:1, 2-- Praise ye the Lord. Praise the Lord, O my soul. 2) While I live will I praise the Lord: I will sing praises unto my God while I have any being. (KJV)

PRAISE DAY 56—I love these words! They touch my soul and they speak to the singer in me. I feel so honored to be allowed to lift up my voice in His praise. Just being able to sing of the mighty God I serve has blessed me in so many ways. It has given me strength when I have felt weak and given me joy in my times of great sorrow.

No one will ever understand the joy I feel when I can sing of his goodness, when I can be a witness to how good God is, when I can speak of God's love that is never ending, when I can let others know God is always on time.

And even when fear and doubts want to try and creep in, God will take all of my fears and doubts away. He has never left me alone and has never allowed me to feel alone.

I can't sing God's praises enough. All I can say is I pray every day that others see Him in me and want to know Him for themselves. I will continue to lift up the Name of the Lord all the days of my life.

There is power in praise! Read Psalm 146 and 150 in their entirety. Also, play or sing one of your favorite songs of praise to our God!

Write your praise report below!

_____

_____

_____

_____

_____

_____

_____

_____

_____

_____

_____

_____

_____

_____

DAY 57

God is My Hope

Psalm 146:5-- Happy is he who has the God of Jacob for his help; Whose hope is in the LORD his God,

PRAISE DAY 57—It is so easy to get distressed about something going on in the world today. There are fires raging out of control while, at the same time, there are floods and hurricanes also taking lives indiscriminately. Daily we are bombarded with news of another tragedy that has taken lives. There are constant reports that lead unsuspecting people to commit some of our most heinous crimes. We might wonder to ourselves if there is any hope.

We have to be mindful of the fact that if these things cause us a bit of distress, how much more will they distress someone who is not in the body of Christ? When you hear someone talking about all of the negative things in the world, share with them that the Lord, our God is our hope! He gives us peace and reassures us that no matter what is going on in the world, all of those things are temporary! The only thing we really need to be focused on is the one thing that is eternal and that is GOD!

Rewrite the above Scripture. Memorize it! The next time you see someone with a distressing look on their face, walk up to them with your biggest, brightest smile and share this Word with them. Not only will it benefit them, but it will benefit you as well! GOD IS MY HOPE!

DAY 58

God is My Joy

Nehemiah 8:10--Then he said to them, "Go your way, eat the fat, drink the sweet, and send portions to those for whom nothing is prepared; for *this* day *is* holy to our Lord. Do not sorrow, for the joy of the LORD is your strength."

PRAISE DAY 58—Not only is the Lord my hope, but He is also my joy and strength. Nehemiah read the Book of the Law to the people of Israel who had returned to Jerusalem after their captivity (Nehemiah 8). After reading the Laws of God, the people were convicted of their sins are became sorrowful (Nehemiah 8:7). Nehemiah encouraged the people, telling them, in essence, don't let these words keep you down!

We are reminded here that although the Word of God does shine a bright light on our weaknesses, failures and sins, God does not convict us in order to embarrass, harass, or condemn us. He does it out of His love for us and His desire for us to be holy!

We can be joyful, even when we have done wrong because our God, our Father, is full of love for us. We only need to repent when He shows us our shortfalls, and return to a right relationship with Him. Because of His forgiving nature, we can find joy in our Lord and in this is our strength to continue in His grace!

Write down those things you need to repent of today! Write them down, repent and rejoice because you have been forgiven. When you find joy in the love and forgiveness of the Lord, there you will also find strength.

Lord, forgive me for I have sinned!

_____

_____

_____

_____

_____

_____

_____

_____

_____

_____

_____

_____

_____

_____

_____

_____

_____

DAY 59

He is Always With Me

I John 4:4—But you belong to God, my dear children. You have already won a victory over those people, because the Spirit who lives in you is greater than the spirit who lives in the world. (NLT)

PRAISE DAY 59— When I read the verse above, I rejoice, knowing that wherever I go, God is with me because His Spirit is in me! If His Spirit is in me, then I have no reason to fear!

According to this Scripture and the previous verses, we have already overcome the enemy, which is Satan! We already have the victory in Christ Jesus! I can rejoice in knowing that the Lord is always with me and I am never alone!

PRAISE REPORT:

_____

_____

_____

_____

_____

_____

DAY 60

This Too Shall Pass

2 Corinthians 4: 17, 18-- **For our light affliction, which is but for a moment, is working for us a far more exceeding and eternal weight of glory, 18) while we do not look at the things which are seen, but at the things which are not seen. For the things which are seen are temporary, but the things which are not seen are eternal.**

PRAISE DAY 60—Sometimes, we just worry about the wrong things in this life! The verse above tells us that everything we can see, touch, taste, experience physically, are all temporary! Yes, and even when we suffer, it is only temporary!

This verse is our encouragement to keep the faith during trying times. We should not put our trust in the temporary things, but our trust should be in God.

We have to fix our hope, our thoughts, our minds, our attitude and our outlook on those things that are eternal! The eternal things such as heaven, reigning with our Lord and Savior Jesus Christ, our resurrected bodies; these are the things that will last through eternity.

Let us praise God this day for everything that we cannot see; those things that are everlasting! AMEN!

Today, go through your house and identify all of the thing that are "temporary"! Your house itself is temporary. Your bills, your car, your bank account and even your body are all temporary! After that, rejoice and praise God for the things that are eternal!

TEMPORARY

_____

_____

_____

_____

_____

_____

ETERNAL

_____

_____

_____

_____

_____

_____

_____

_____

_____

DAY 61

Things Could Be Worse

Psalm 34:19-- For Many are the afflictions of the righteous, But the LORD delivers him out of them all.

PRAISE DAY 61—So, you think you have problems! Guess what? We all do! We often feel as if we are the only ones who are suffering with our type of problems. We sometimes feel as if no one knows our struggles. We think that perhaps God has left us and we don't know why. Let me share this with you; God has never promised that we would not have problems, but He did promise to deliver us out of them!

There is a man that I know of who had a massive stroke. The stroke was so debilitating that the only part of his body he had control of is his eyes! For 15 years he laid on his bed unable to eat, unable to speak, and unable to take care of himself. For years, Christians surrounded his bed, praying that the Lord would bless him, heal him and at least allowing him to speak.

Recently, the prayers of the righteous ones were answered! The man was blessed with an extremely expensive piece of technology that would allow him to send emails and text messages by the movement of his eyes! You would think that the man would send messages of doom, gloom and despair, but the opposite is true! He constantly sends out messages of hope in Christ Jesus and messages to encourage those who might be struggling or hurting! Can you imagine? Even on his bed of affliction, this man still praises God! And you thought you had problems! Realize today that no matter your situation, there is always someone worse off than you!

Rejoice not only in your current state, but praise God for allowing your eyes to be opened and pray for the ones God will lead you to who have greater needs than you! You will find that in blessing them, God is blessing you!

Contributed by Ethel "Mother" Ellis

PRAISE REPORT:

_____

_____

_____

_____

_____

_____

_____

_____

_____

_____

DAY 62

I am on God's Mind

Psalm 40:17--For But I *am* poor and needy;
Yet the LORD thinks upon me.
You *are* my help and my deliverer;
Do not delay, O my God.

PRAISE DAY 62—Who am I that the Lord would have me on His mind? What makes me so special to Him that He would think about me? What do I have that would make me important enough for me to come to the Lord's remembrance? I am nothing! My sins are great! The hairs on my head can't out number my iniquities! I am like a poor and needy person with nothing to offer but in need of so much!

This is the picture David was trying to paint in this particular Psalm. Just reading it would make us feel miserable because of our poverty in the eyes of God. However, before David closes out this Psalm, he writes the word "YET" which is synonymous to BUT. He points out that despite all of these things I think about myself, "the Lord thinks upon me."

Not only does He think about me, but He knows me better than I know myself. And lastly, what God already knows about me is far more important than what others *think* they know about me and even what I think I know about myself!

Because of that, what God thinks matters and nothing else does! And so, I can rejoice!

PRAISE REPORT:

_____

_____

_____

_____

_____

_____

_____

_____

_____

_____

_____

_____

_____

_____

_____

_____

DAY 63

Thank God for Jesus

Romans 5:17-- For if by the one man's offense death reigned through the one, much more those who receive abundance of grace and of the gift of righteousness will reign in life through the One, Jesus Christ.

PRAISE **DAY 63**—No other religious leader has a RESUME' like JESUS! Job Qualifications include but are not limited to: Healer, Deliverer, Judge, Priest, Miracle Worker, Missionary, Feeder of Thousands, Great with Mathematics (Able to feed 5,000 with two fish and five loaves), Counselor, Righteous, True, Everlasting, Faithful (Once accepted in the position of your Lord and Savior, He will never leave you!), Trustworthy, Creator, Provider, Shepherd, Keeper, Redeemer, and (oh, yeah) KING of kings, LORD of lords, Lord and Savior, MIGHTY in BATTLE, PRINCE of Peace, ALL THAT I NEED AND MORE!!!

Song writers say it like this:

1. He is my joy in sorrow, hope for tomorrow
2. My beginning and He's my end
3. He is my Peace
4. He is my Hope
5. Searched all over and couldn't find anybody greater

6. There's none like Him

7. He's my everything

8. Mary's Baby, born in a manger

9. Son of God

10. My water in dry places

11. My shield and protection

12. He is my righteousness

Who/What is Jesus to you? Praise God for Who Jesus is!

DAY 64

He Comforts Me

John 14:16--"And I will pray the Father, and He will give you another Helper (*Comforter*), that He may abide with you forever—

PRAISE DAY 64—In the Scripture above, the King James Version uses the word "comforter" and the New King James Version uses the word "helper", as to identify the Holy Spirit. When I read this verse, it reminds me of my children when they were smaller and how, when they wanted to be comforted, they would stand before me (or my husband), lift up their hands and wait with eager anticipation as we lowered our hands to raise them up. Often, they would be satisfied and reassured after a few brief moments in our arms. Then they would be ready again to tackle any task that is set before them.

There are times in our Christian walk where we feel just like my children did and still do. Every now and then we just need a hug from the Lord! Follow the directions that we have received from our children. Stand (or bow) before the Lord with outstretched arms, with our heads lifted towards heaven. Wait with eager anticipation. He will lower His arms and lift our spirits! He will guide and comfort you as you tackle whatever tasks set before you.

The Holy Spirit is our "comforter" and fits like a warm blanket on a cold winter's night. Praise the Lord, our Comforter and our Keeper!

_____

_____

_____

_____

_____

_____

_____

_____

_____

_____

_____

_____

_____

_____

_____

_____

_____

DAY 65

Goodness and Mercy Follow Me

Psalm 23:6a-- Surely goodness and mercy shall follow me all the days of my life

PRAISE DAY 65—This verse has been a major part of my entire life. I like to call it those Heavenly Twins, GRACE and Mercy. Yes GRACE and MERCY have been with me all of my 55 years. They first came into my life at the time of my birth when a decision was made for me to live with my grandmother. We grew up "po" but never knew it. My grandmother did not make much money on her housecleaning job but we never missed a meal. We always had nice clean clothes. We went to church every Sunday and my grandmother never missed a tithe. Growing up, as a child, from time to time I got into various situations where there could have been serious injury to me but again GRACE and MERCY was right there to protect me.

As I became an adult I really began to identify what GRACE and MERCY really meant. In college when I did not deserve to graduate, GRACE and MERCY stepped in and allowed me to graduate. When I was looking for a stable job, Grace and MERCY allowed me to find a job where I would make my career for 31 years and counting. In this job I moved to five different cities. Each time GRACE and MERCY was right there to assure a smooth transition. When I lost my first two children to an early death, GRACE and MERCY allowed three other children to come forth. I have had several visits to hospitals for different reasons, each time GRACE and MERCY was right there to bring me through.

I will be extremely thankful to GOD for blessing me with GRACE and MERCY. GOD has been extremely good to me throughout my journey. HE has been so gracious to provide those HEAVENLY TWINS as my constant helpers and I could not have been in better hands. Believe me there have been many dark days and I have no doubts without my HEAVENLY TWINS I would not have made it and I have no doubt they will follow me all the days of my life.

Contributed by
Christopher Michael Zepher

Now, take a few moments and write down at least one time in your life where you knew it was only because of God's grace and mercy that you "made it"!

Write your praise report below!

_____

_____

_____

_____

_____

_____

_____

_____

_____

_____

_____

_____

_____

_____

_____

DAY 66

My Hedge of Protection

Job 1:10--"Have You not made a hedge around him, around his household, and around all that he has on every side? You have blessed the work of his hands, and his possessions have increased in the land.

PRAISE DAY 66— During my reading and study of the book of Job, I came to realize that the devil can only do so much to us! Before Satan could activate his plan against Job, in order to get Job to turn away from God, he had to have permission (Job Ch. 1)! Satan indicated that he would ruin Job's world, only if the Lord would remove the hedge of protection that He had placed around Job. Even though the Lord agreed to remove the hedge, He explicitly forbade the enemy from "touching Job's life" (Job 2:4).

Even though God allowed Satan to take so much from Job, Satan was still limited in his actions against Job. Even with us today, the Lord has a hedge of protection around us. The things the Satan conjures up in his mind have to be approved by the Lord before the he can execute his plan. So, with that being said and declared, I can rest assured in knowing that the things that I am going through are only the things that God allows!

Praise God for His protection!

Pray for God's protection and then Praise Him because you are protected! There are many companies in the world that provide us with "insurance"; God gives Christians His blessed "assurance".

_____

_____

_____

_____

_____

_____

_____

_____

_____

_____

_____

_____

_____

_____

_____

_____

_____

_____

_____

DAY 67

Wait On the Lord

Psalm 27:14—Wait on the LORD; Be of good courage, And He shall strengthen your heart; Wait, I say, on the LORD!

PRAISE DAY 67— There may be a time in your life where you feel as if you are running in mud! You may have been or may be fasting and praying, talking to the Lord and waiting for your much needed answer. The first thing you have to realize is that God heard you the first time! When we pray according to His will in our lives, He is already in the process of delivering us the answer to our prayers!

There will be times when we will have to wait for it. There will be times when the Lord will have to put in a preparation mode. Additionally, there will be times when He will have to prepare other people, places and things before we can attain what we have been praying for.

The problem is not in our prayer (most of the time), but it is in the waiting! We pray and we want our *cake* as soon as we ask for it! We forget that the mix has to be prepared and the cake has to be baked in the oven! Instead of waiting impatiently as if we *watching* the cake bake; wait on the Lord as if you are waiting on the surprise birthday party! Expect, anticipate and praise Him for what He is already doing!

_____

_____

_____

_____

_____

_____

_____

_____

_____

_____

_____

_____

_____

_____

_____

_____

_____

_____

DAY 68

It is Well With My Soul

Psalm 104:1-- For Bless the LORD, O my soul!
O LORD my God, You are very great:
You are clothed with honor and majesty,

Psalm 107:9-- For He satisfies the longing soul,
And fills the hungry soul with goodness.

PRAISE **DAY 68**—There is a popular hymn that was written by Horatio Spafford and composed by Philip Bliss. It was first published in 1876. The title of the hymn is "It is well with My Soul" and the words for the first verse are:

When peace like a river, attendeth my way,

When sorrows like sea billows roll;

Whatever my lot, Thou hast taught me to <u>know</u>,

It is well, it is well, with my soul.

<u>*Refrain:*</u>

It is well, (it is well),

With my soul, (with my soul)

It is well, it is well, with my soul.

The amazing thing to me about this hymn is the fact that Spafford, according to Wikipedia references, wrote these words after suffering the loss of his business, his fortune and his four daughters were also lost when their ship, traveling to Europe, collided with another ship and sank. In the presence of his tragedy, Spafford found peace within his soul. I imagine that this is a peace that can only come from and through our faith in God.

There may be some of you who are reading this praise journal because of a great tragedy that you have suffered. As Christians, we suffer as any other person, however, we should find our peace in Christ Jesus! As our Scriptures above state, God is still great, even when we are burdened and He will fill our souls with His goodness.

Praise God in the middle of your sorrows, for the restoration of your joy!

_____

_____

_____

_____

_____

_____

_____

_____

_____

_____

_____

DAY 69

Prayer and Praise Closet

Matthew 6:6-- "But you, when you pray, go into your room, and when you have shut your door, pray to your Father who *is* in the secret *place*; and your Father who sees in secret will reward you openly.

PRAISE DAY 69—In September of 2015, the Kendrick Brothers released a faith based film entitles, "War Room". The essence of the movie showed the importance in the life of a Christian to have a prayer room or a space in their home designated as the location where they pray. In the movie, the prayer room for one of the characters was her closet. The closet was void of clothes and was only used by her for prayer. There, in her "secret place", she laid her petitions before the Lord. She put Scriptures up on the wall of the closet that supported her faith in her prayers.

The prayer room or closet is not a new idea, but a modern twist to something that Christ established a long time ago! See the Scripture above? It tells us to, "go into your room, and when you have shut your door (get some privacy), pray…"! I encourage you: after you pray and before you leave your prayer closet or room, don't forget to give God some praise! Thank Him in advance for what you believe He will do for you!

If you don't have one already, locate a place in your home where you can pray in private, without any distractions. Put your favorite (and maybe not so favorite) Scriptures on the wall. Maybe make a "Prayer Wall" and include a listing of all of the people, places and/things you are praying about. Your prayer space can be a closet, a bedroom, your study, your bathroom, or any other place where you can spend some quiet time with the Lord. Let your family know that when you are in your "room" that you are not to be disturbed! Pray then Praise!

WHERE IS YOUR PRAYER AND PRAISE SPACE?

_____

_____

_____

_____

_____

_____

_____

_____

_____

_____

_____

DAY 70

God's Plan for Me

Psalm 139:16-- For Your eyes saw my substance, being yet
  unformed.
  And in Your book they all were written,
  The days fashioned for me,
  When *as yet there were* none of them.

PRAISE DAY 70—Do you realize that every day of your life is already written in the Lord's book? The NIV translates the verse above like this: "Your eyes saw my unformed body; all the days ordained for me were written in your book before one of them came to be." Every day, every blessing, every trial, every triumph, every gift, every relationship—everything!

The question becomes, then why am I so depressed? The answer is simple: God allows us to make the choice to live the life that He has planned for us or to live the way we want to. I call that, "Living off the page." Think about your parents and the things that they "planned" for you. Did you obey their every command and submit yourself to their every plan? Think about your children. Have they done everything you wanted them to do and turned out exactly the way you figured they would? That's because no matter what you may want for them, they still—just as you—make up their own minds and make decisions for themselves.

These decisions we make on our own, without consulting God first, will lead us down roads of despair! When we end up in a situation that causes us to suffer, we only have to look to the Lord! We can rejoice in knowing that no matter how far "off the page" we have strayed, the "book" is still intact and we can return to where we are supposed to be by simply surrendering to the will of God. As a song writer once said, "the safest place in this whole wide world is in the will of God"!

COMMIT TO SUBMIT TODAY!

DAY 71

Praise God in the Congregation

Psalm 111:1 -- Praise the LORD!
I will praise the LORD with *my* whole heart,
In the assembly of the upright and *in* the
congregation.

PRAISE DAY 71—How do you feel when you are at your church? How do you feel when you leave your church? Are fired up? Have you been restored? Have you been revived? Or, do you feel the same way when you leave as you did when you came?

Some, who feel no different when they leave the church on Sundays after their church services, have a tendency to blame the pastor or the choir. Many people get frustrated with the atmosphere of their church that they either stop coming or they change churches. As the above verse points out, we all are responsible for praise in our churches!

The Psalmist Writes the command; "Praise the Lord!" According to what English teachers across the land, whenever a sentence starts with a verb (PRAISE), there is an "understood YOU" at the beginning of that sentence. Therefore, the first sentence more accurately expresses, "**YOU** praise the Lord!"

We are given further instructions to praise God in the

congregation! That means when we come to church, we should be prepared, beforehand, to do our part in the worship of our God! We should praise God with all of our hearts! We should give God the same energy, if you will, during the worship service as we give football players during a football game! So, go ahead! On the next Sunday when you find yourself in church, sing, shout, dance, clap your hands, lift your voice and Praise the LORD!

Write Your Congregational Praise Experience Below!

_____

_____

_____

_____

_____

_____

_____

_____

_____

_____

_____

_____

_____

_____

_____

DAY 72

Sing of His Wonderful Works

I Chronicles 16:9—Sing to Him, sing psalms to Him; Talk of all His wondrous works!

PRAISE DAY 72—We talk all the time. It's our nature as human beings and our desire to communicate. There is no problem with communicating. The problem is in what we communicate about! Have you ever noticed that the more you talk about a particular thing, the bigger that thing or issue seems to get? The problem grows like a snowball rolling down a snow covered hillside! It grows and grows until it is impossible to stop!

Your challenge today is to avoid negative communication, coming from you or other people. Instead of the negative, accentuate and lift up the positive! Talk about the wondrous works of our Lord! Talk about His goodness and His promises! Talk about the great things He has done, not only in your life but in the lives of others.

Don't talk about *your* problems, *your* issues, *your* sickness, *your* weaknesses or *your* disputes! It's not about you anyway! It's all about *HIM*!

What can you tell someone about God's Wonderful works? Rejoice! Praise Him! Write it down so that when the time comes, you will be ready!

_____

_____

_____

_____

_____

_____

_____

_____

_____

_____

_____

_____

_____

_____

_____

DAY 73

He Has Delivered Me

Psalm 34:4-- I sought the LORD, and He heard me, and delivered me from all my fears.

PRAISE **DAY** 73—When you were younger, were you ever at home alone, especially during the evening when it was dark? Did it seem to you as if everything in the house was alive and making noises? How did you feel? What about in the middle of the night when everyone else was asleep and for some reason or another you found yourself wide awake, afraid to leave your bed because of the darkness that awaited you on the other side of your bedroom door? Ever fear the "monster in the closet" or the one under the bed?

What about as an adult? Fear changing jobs? Do you Fear buying a new home or getting a new vehicle? What about moving to an entirely new location? Getting a higher education? Starting a new or your own business? Writing a book? Do those thoughts frighten you? Is your fear immobilizing your faith? Well, the solution is as plain as the nose on your face! As our Scripture points out, seek the Lord in prayer! Allow Him to direct you and He will deliver you from the fear! There are many times when our fears are nothing more than **F**alse **E**vidence **A**ppearing **R**eal!

What would you do if money and time were no object and if you knew you wouldn't fail? Would you get more education? Start that business you've been thinking about for years? What? Write it down, pray and then praise! If it is the Lord's will, allow Him to direct you. If it is not in His will, then allow Him to remove the desire from you! Either way, your fear will be gone! Stop dreaming and start doing! Praise God!

_____

_____

_____

_____

_____

_____

_____

_____

_____

_____

_____

_____

_____

_____

_____

DAY 74

He Makes My Enemies My Footstool

Psalm 110:1-- A Psalm of David.
   The LORD said to my Lord,
   "Sit at My right hand,
   Till I make Your enemies Your footstool."

PRAISE DAY 74—What do we do when it seems as if "all hell is breaking loose"? We try to work it out, pay things out, think it out, worry about circumstances that we can't begin to describe and more! We try to pray more and only end up feeling more frustrated. Then, in turn, we stop praying altogether, thinking that our prayers are going unheard and unanswered.

We read in the tenth chapter of the Book of Daniel, where Daniel prayed for several days and he was in despair because he had not received an answer. A few verses later, we read where an Angel shows up and responds to Daniel, telling him that as soon as he prayed his words were heard, but the enemy caused him, the angel, to be detained until he received assistance from the Angel Michael (Daniel 10:10-13).

This reminds us that God hears when we pray and we have to trust that when He hears us, He is working things out for us. As a result of our faith in our prayers, we can rest with assurance that our situation is in God's hands.

While you are resting, you can give a shout of praise to God because He has no problem putting the enemy in his place! And, the only place the enemy, that is Satan, has in the life of a Christian is that small space between your foot and the ground!

PRAISE REPORT:

_____

_____

_____

_____

_____

_____

_____

_____

_____

_____

_____

_____

_____

_____

_____

_____

DAY 75

While I Live

Psalm 146:1, 2—Oh Praise ye the Lord. Praise the Lord, O my soul. While I live will I praise the Lord: I will sing praises unto my God while I have any being. (KJV)

PRAISE DAY 75—I love these words they touch my soul and they speak to the singer in me. I feel so honored to be allowed to lift up my voice in praise. Just being able to sing of the mighty God I serve has blessed me in so many ways. It has given me strength when I have felt weak and given me joy in my times of great sorrow.

No one will ever understand the joy I feel when I can sing of His goodness, when I can be a witness to how good God is, when I can speak of God's love that is never ending and when I can let others know God is always on time.

Even when fear and doubts want to try and creep in God will take all your fears and doubts away, and for me, how He has never left me alone and has never allowed me to feel alone. I can't God sing praise enough all I can say is I pray every day that other see him in me and want to know him for themselves. I will continue to lift up the name of the Lord all the days of my life.

Contributed by Bridgette Moore

Pull out your favorite Christian music artist or turn on your favorite Christian music station on either the radio or TV network. You could also search the web for your favorite Christian songs or hymns. Or, you could play the praise CD that you made for yourself at the beginning of this book!

How are you feeling after listening to and perhaps joining in on the singing of praises? Write your praise report!

_____

_____

_____

_____

_____

_____

_____

_____

_____

_____

_____

_____

_____

DAY 76

God is My Rock

Psalm 95:1—Oh come, let us sing to the LORD! Let us shout joyfully to the Rock of our salvation.

PRAISE DAY 76—Any construction worker will tell you that when there are cracks in the walls of a house, most likely, the problem is with the foundation! And, in order to fix the cracks in the wall, one would have to start with the repairs on the foundation.

Jesus even used the parable found in Matthew 7:24, where we find the story about the wise and the foolish men. In that parable, Jesus states, "Therefore whoever hears these sayings of Mine, and does them, I will liken him to a wise man who built his house on the rock:" In the following verses He shares that the foolish man who builds his house upon the sand, or an unstable foundation, is bound to fall down, and even mightily so, in a storm.

As this entire parable points out, whether we build on the Rock or on the sand, there will be storms we will have to face. The problem is not the storm, but the foundation upon which your faith is built! We, as Christians, can rejoice and praise God because He is our Rock, which is the foundation upon which we stand. We have the assurance of God who is ever our Tower of strength.

PRAISE REPORT

DAY 77

I Think Myself Happy

Philippians 4:8—Finally, brethren, whatever things are true, whatever things are noble, whatever things are just, whatever things are pure, whatever things are lovely, whatever things are of good report, if there is any virtue and if there is anything praiseworthy—meditate on these things.

PRAISE DAY 77—There is so much going on in the world today that it is easy to understand why so many people feel as if there is nothing good any more. Paul said, "I think myself happy," in Acts 26:2 when he was allowed to speak for himself before King Agrippa, however, thinking myself happy goes beyond Paul's reference. While he was being accused of all manner of evil, he was happy about the opportunities to not only speak about his innocence, but he was able to share the Gospel of Jesus Christ along with his testimony of salvation. It is in times of grief where we can give this suffering world hope.

We can share "whatever things are true, whatever things are noble, whatever things are just, whatever things are pure, whatever things are lovely, whatever things are of good report, if there is any virtue and if there is anything praiseworthy," as our Scripture above states. And, all of these things can be summed up in one Name—

Jesus Christ! Not only can we *think* on Him, but <u>meditate</u> on Him! He is in the beginning and He is in the ending, so everything in the middle really doesn't matter! Rejoice in our Eternal Christ Jesus for one day, we will reign with Him!

PRAISE REPORT:

_____

_____

_____

_____

_____

_____

_____

_____

_____

_____

_____

_____

_____

_____

_____

DAY 78

My Soul Magnifies the Lord

Luke 1:46, 47—And Mary said: "My soul magnifies the Lord, 47) and my spirit has rejoiced in God my Savior."

PRAISE DAY 78—If you have ever been given an opportunity to do something great, chances are you can somewhat relate to Mary in the above verses of Scripture. You probably realized that you were unworthy, that you didn't have all of the skills and/or knowledge you would need in order to perform that task at hand. Nevertheless, you accepted the challenge with great humility, trusting that whatever you needed, God would somehow provide it.

There will be times when God will use you to do something for Him that is extraordinary! These astonishing things would be above your own abilities and strength and would require faith and obedience. The Lord doesn't expect you to have all of the answers! He expects you to seek Him and ask Him for the answers! He will use you to do something that you are incapable of doing by yourself because He wants you to depend on Him. God uses ordinary people to do extra ordinary things!

Praise God for the amazing things He is about to do through you!

PRAISE REPORT:

DAY 79

He Makes Me Strong

II Corinthians 12:10-- Therefore I take pleasure in infirmities, in reproaches, in needs, in persecutions, in distresses, for Christ's sake. For when I am weak, then I am strong.

PRAISE DAY 79—When I see this verse, it reminds me of my worst days! You know, those days where everything seems to be going wrong. You wake up late, the children miss the school bus, you forget to give them lunch money, you speed trying to get to work only to be stopped by a police officer and all of this happens before 8:00 in the morning!

Then, things continue to spiral downward! It starts raining, you can't find a parking spot so you have to park too far from your work location, you get drenched while running to the building and just as you enter the building and think you are going to be okay, you slip and fall on the floor in front of all of your co-workers! On top of that, your boss sees you entering the building late!

And, just as you are about to run to the restroom and hide for the rest of the day, the words, "when I am weak, then I am strong," resonate in your mind and spirit! Instead of running, you walk to the restroom to regain your composure and pray. While you are praying, someone brings you a towel and perhaps something dry

---

to cover up with. Another co-worker says he will help you catch up with your duties for the day. Later on you call the school about the lunch money and learn that the lunches are paid for because you have been paying extra! The more you begin to proceed through your day, the things that were designed to cause you to be weak in your faith are the very things God will turn around to make you strong!

As Paul says in preceding verse found in II Corinthians 12:9, "And He said to me, 'My grace is sufficient for you, for My strength is made perfect in weakness.' Therefore most gladly I will rather boast in my infirmities, that the power of Christ may rest upon me." We can rejoice, knowing that God will use our weaknesses to make us strong!

PRAISE REPORT:

_____

_____

_____

_____

_____

_____

_____

_____

DAY 80

Chasing Thousands

Joshua 23:10— "One man of you shall chase a thousand, for the LORD your God is He who fights for you, as He promised you."

PRAISE DAY 80—If it has not happened already, there will be times in your life where you feel as if your problems or circumstances are coming upon you like the weight of a thousand men. This weight can be in the form of financial problems, marital problems, issues with your children or even health or medical concerns. You may feel as if you are surrounded by your enemy and you are about to be consumed in the misery of your trouble.

As this Word above promises, the Lord our God is the One who fights for us! He is our victory! He is our deliverer! He is our strength! And, with the Lord on our side, we can chase thousands! So, stand up! Be firm! It is your house; it is your life! Now, turn your issues and concerns over to the Lord and allow Him to fight the battle for you!

While He is working things out on your behalf, you have to do your part and anticipate His deliverance. Walk by faith, expecting doors to open, expect to see something or someone that will benefit your situation. Believe that God is arranging an answer for you! Prepare to receive the blessing. Praise Him while you are waiting!

PRAISE REPORT:

_____

_____

_____

_____

_____

_____

_____

_____

_____

_____

_____

_____

_____

_____

_____

_____

_____

_____

DAY 81

God is Love

I John 4:16—And we have known and believed the love that God has for us. God is love, and he who abides in love abides in God, and God in him.

PRAISE DAY 81—When I think about the love of God, the verse above comes to mind. The part that really stands out is the words "God is love". His love is incomparable, forgiving, and it is a love that covers a multitude of sins. This verse goes on to say that if I abide in the love of God, then He also abides in me!

The words that are found in the 13th chapter of First Corinthians encompass the entirety of God's love. That section of Scripture starts out by saying that my very words have to be wrapped in love; otherwise I'm just making a loud noise with my mouth. So, that reassures me that every word out of the mouth of God is spoken out of love for me!

This great love chapter goes on to say that everything I do, whether it is giving to the poor, all of my attempts at increasing my intellect, and even my faith have to be a product of love. If not, I have wasted too much energy trying to accomplish and obtain things that will not last. The last verse of the Scripture tells me that the greatest gift that one can obtain is an unconditional love for self, for God and for mankind.

The last verse says, "And now abide faith, hope, love, these three; but the greatest of these is love." Thank and praise God for His love towards us. He loves us so much that while we were in sin, He sent Jesus to be our Savior. Knowing that God has this kind of love for me and knowing that He had me in mind when He created me, gives me reason to give Him praise!

And for that reason, we can praise Him because He first loved us.

DAY 82

I am the Lord's Witness

Acts 4:33—And with great power the apostles gave witness to the resurrection of the Lord Jesus. And great grace was upon them all.

PRAISE DAY 82—How do you represent our Christ? What does your "witness" say about you? What does your witness say about Christ? Your witness can be found in the way you walk and even as importantly, the way you talk! Does your life line up with the words that are coming out of your mouth? Do your words line up with the Word of the Lord?

John's Gospel in chapter 1, verse 18 says that we have been given "power" to become sons (and daughters) of God! Because His Spirit dwells in us, leads us, guides and directs us, we are equipped to live our lives in a holy manner. However, we still have the ability to make our own choices. As Christians, our lives should exemplify Christ!

PRAISE REPORT:

_____

_____

_____

_____

DAY 83

Love Your Enemies

Luke 6:35—"But love your enemies, do good, and lend, hoping for nothing in return; and your reward will be great, and you will be sons of the Most High. For He is kind to the unthankful and evil.

PRAISE DAY 83—We stress over things and people that Christ has instructed us to forgive and love.

We say it all the time! This person or that person makes me angry! Situations are neutral. Our responses to situations make them either positive or negative. People can't *make* us angry. We decide to be angry because of a given person or situation.

God will not hold us responsible for the way people treat us, but He will hold us responsible for the way we treat them!

For He is kind even to those who are unthankful and evil. I know it doesn't seem right! In our small minds, it *isn't* right! That's why we can be thankful and praise God even in these situations because He has given us another opportunity to be merciful! Being merciful entails forgiving those we think do not deserve our forgiveness. By our being merciful and showing mercy, we are exemplifying *Him*! "*Be merciful, as your Father is merciful* (Matthew 5:48). My reward is in Heaven anyway!

Make a list of people, things and/or situations that you have been angry about. You may have been angry for years, even if that person is deceased! Now is time for you to let those things go. Give them to Jesus, and rejoice because you have been delivered from your anger!

_____

_____

_____

_____

_____

_____

_____

_____

_____

_____

_____

_____

_____

DAY 84

Incomprehensible Peace

Philippians 4:7-- and the peace of God, which surpasses all understanding, will guard your hearts and minds through Christ Jesus.

PRAISE DAY 84—Living as a Christian is not always easy! There is so much that one has to deal with on a daily basis, not including the attitudes and personalities of those we encounter! Any atmosphere itself can be a very negative, and our place of employment can be a very hostile environment to work in. Sometimes, it is hard for us to believe that we have done it—stayed in the same job or even the same marriage—for over twenty years or more!

When people see me, most of the time I have a smile on my face. I am often asked, "How can you smile day after day, working in this place?" Some have even said to me that even on the worst days, I can still be found with a smile on my face.

I simply smile even more and reply, "JESUS!" If I am asked for more information, I provide the inquisitive one with the Scripture above. I let them know that the smile on my face is the outward sign that I have inner peace.

I pray that you will receive the peace of God today!

SHARE A SMILE TODAY!

_____

_____

_____

_____

_____

_____

_____

_____

_____

_____

_____

_____

_____

_____

_____

_____

_____

DAY 85

Unspeakable Joy

I Peter 1:8, 9-- I Peter 1:8, 9--Whom having not seen, ye love; in whom, though now ye see him not, yet believing, ye rejoice with joy unspeakable and full of glory: 9) Receiving the end of your faith, even the salvation of your souls. (KJV)

PRAISE DAY 85—Working in an adult correctional facility can be a depressing environment. To see so many people incarcerated for everything from check writing to mass murder, not knowing who committed what offense, would make anyone apprehensive about life in general. The question that one might ask over and over is, "What made them do what they did?"

One of the reasons that I can maintain a level of joy is because I know who walks with me! Jesus! I don't have to allow my surroundings dictate my attitude about where I work! I don't have to let my circumstances influence my emotions. The reason for my strength can be found in the fact that I know who holds my present, my past and my future! God knows my coming and going! I trust Him to take me to my work location and bring me home at the end of the day. The smile on my face is the outward sign that I have inner peace and joy!

If you can't change your situation, change your attitude about it! If you are not happy with your job, get excited by the fact that you are getting paid! If your check is not enough, thank God for providing you with everything you need beyond your check! Also, thank Him for blessing you (in advance) with good budgeting skills! Thank Him because things could always be worse than they are!

LORD, THANK YOU FOR YOUR INNER PEACE!

_____

_____

_____

_____

_____

_____

_____

_____

_____

_____

_____

_____

_____

DAY 86

Run! Tell That!

John 4:28-29—The woman then left her waterpot, went her way into the city, and said to the men, "Come, see a Man who told me all things that I ever did. Could this be the Christ?"

PRAISE DAY 86—There is a story in the Bible about a woman at the well, found in the fourth chapter of John. In this story, this unnamed woman has a personal encounter with Jesus. After her encounter, she is so excited that she dropped her water pot and ran into the city (I imagine she ran because she "left her water pot" which signifies that she was in a hurry, as well as excited). She tells her story to the men about her meeting (verses 28-30). She was so convincing that the men came to Jesus for their own personal experience.

What is your story? What is your personal encounter with Jesus Christ? What experience have you had whereby you knew that without a doubt that God delivered you? When was the last time you prayed about something and God answered your prayer? What have you believed the Lord for and He delivered it? Think about a time that excited you so much that you had to run and tell it!

It is so easy to share bad news; just look at some of the post on social media! Now, let's turn that around and share something

GOOD!!!

Write down your miracle and/or blessing!

_____

_____

_____

_____

_____

_____

_____

_____

_____

Now, identify five people you will share this miracle with within the next 24 hours! Don't be afraid to share what God has done for you! It will bless somebody!

1. _____

2. _____

3. _____

4. _____

5. _____

DAY 87

I am Thankful

Psalm 100:4-- For Enter into His gates with thanksgiving,
And into His courts with praise.
Be thankful to Him, *and* bless His name.

PRAISE DAY 87—For some people, the Thanksgiving Holiday is a time to pause and reflect about all that one is thankful for. People think about and find unique ways to display their thanks. They will list things like family, children, spouse, jobs, health and finances. But the Scripture above wants us to pause and reflect on more than just the physical things. We should also be thankful for the spiritual things that only God can provide!

Not only should we think about the spiritual things, but we should do so more than that one time per year! Our thanks should begin ever time we enter into the church, every time we enter into a place of worship. We should be thankful and verbalize our thanks every time we come before Him to worship, such as in our prayer time! We spend too much time in prayer, asking God to fix our circumstances and not enough time thanking Him for His spirit!

So, today, take a few moments and thank God and be full of thanks for the things that money can't buy and that only He can give! Things like peace, joy, stable mind, grace, favor, mercy, His faithfulness, His presence, truth, protection from dangers we see and those we can't see, blessed assurance, covering, hedge of protection, sense of belonging, love everlasting and so much more! Make your list below:

_____

_____

_____

_____

_____

_____

_____

_____

_____

_____

_____

_____

_____

_____

_____

_____

_____

DAY 88

My Refuge

Psalm 91:2-- For I will say of the LORD, "He is my refuge and my fortress; My God, in Him I will trust."

PRAISE DAY 88—It was pouring down rain outside. As I prepared to leave work headed for the house, all I could think about was the long drive home. Typically these types of days lead to wrecks, traffic jams and irresponsible drivers on the roadways. I walked to my car praying, "Lord Jesus your traveling grace please." I got into the car the whole while having a conversation with my Father, reminding Him of His promise to always take care of me, to let no evil befall me, for He was my refuge. Traffic was a nightmare so I decided to put in one of my Praise and Worship CD's elevating to higher ground.

As I crept along the freeway my phone started ringing. It was my sister calling. She told me she just called 911 for mom, they were there now. My heart started pumping and I immediately went into prayer mode; I found myself 2 exits from her house so I rushed to see what was going on. When I pulled up to the house, they were loading mom into the ambulance. She didn't look like anything was wrong, no pain that I could determine. We got to the ER where they examined her, ran a lot of test, lab work etc... All came back clean but they wanted to admit her for more test. As we waited for a room, my life line kept creeping into my spirit and I found myself leaning heavily upon it.

> *I will say of the LORD, He is my refuge and my fortress: my God; in him will I trust.*

> *Surely he shall deliver thee from the snare of the fowler, and from the noisome pestilence.*

> *He shall cover thee with his feathers, and under his wings shalt thou trust: his truth shall be thy shield and buckler. Thou shalt not be afraid for the terror by night; nor for the arrow that flieth by day;*

Once in the room, mom became restless and my sister Phyllis was going to stay the night. We decided we would alternate never leaving her there alone. They did a colonoscopy the next day and found nothing, mom was bleeding from the Colon yet they could not pinpoint where. The doctor decided to keep her one more day for yet another test called a bleed test. Weary, tired and frustrated I left the hospital headed home, in the driveway of my house I sat, looking at nothing yet in deep concentration talking to my Father. I asked Him to fix it, and went into the house. While lying in bed later that night He responded:

> *Because thou hast made the LORD, which is my refuge, even the most High, thy habitation; there shall no evil befall thee, neither shall any plague come nigh thy dwelling.*

My phone rang about 2am it was my sister, once again I immediately went into prayer mode. She said mom was bleeding again, lost a lot of blood, they were doing a transfusion, and then moving her to ICU, this went on for 3 days, they did several test and could not find where the bleeding was coming from. The doctor called us together to say the last option would be to remove the colon, I responded, not an option. I called on my prayer warriors, I knew at that moment we were in a spiritual battle, it was time for war. I kept repeating this verse:

A thousand shall fall at thy side, and ten thousand at thy right hand; but it shall not come nigh thee.

See, I wanted the devil to know what I knew, and had to put him on notice; not this day Satan nor this woman. Mom was restless while in ICU, they had to give her yet another transfusion and decided to put a central line in because her IV in her veins were not capable of bearing the weight of the blood. As she laid there asleep I couldn't help but think how vulnerable she looked, I almost started having a pity party, (see Satan strikes at your weak moments). Notice I said, "Almost," because at that precise time my phone rang (God is good and knows what we need and when we need it, always right on time). It was one of my prayer partners, (not today devil!!)

We talked and prayed and I reminded God of how good He is and I started thankful mode. I thanked Him for His angels encamped around mom keeping the enemy at bay; they were trying to take her out but Hey!!!! Hallelujah! Could not get to her…

For he shall give his angels charge over thee, to keep thee in all thy ways. They shall bear thee up in their hands, lest thou dash thy foot against a stone.

I prayed Lord Jesus, I know You got this, I trust in You not what my eyes see nor my ears hear. They could not pinpoint the source of the blood, so I need You Father, to plug it, stop it from flowing… That was 9 days ago and still no bleeding. I will continue to trust Him for what He had done and continue to do. Psalms 91 is my daily bread; it is a constant in my life. I know I always have a hiding place when life gets to rough. I know God has promised to take care of me and shield me, I know I do not walk alone; His angels are encamped all around me. I know if He can do it for me, He can and will do it you. Thank You, Jesus for Your Faithfulness.

Contributed by Gwendolyn Jones

When we need a refuge, a safe haven, a place of shelter, there is no one greater than the Lord! He will shield and protect us and the ones we love! Praise Him for keeping you in times of great distress! He is our sanctuary!

PRAISE REPORT:

_____

_____

_____

_____

_____

_____

_____

_____

_____

_____

_____

_____

_____

_____

_____

_____

_____

_____

_____

DAY 89

Praise Him for Righteousness

Psalm 35:28—And my tongue shall speak of Your righteousness And of Your praise all the day long.

PRAISE DAY 89—If you have ever been falsely accused of doing something or not doing something, you are not alone! It happens, even to us Christians, all the time. When something has gone awry in the workplace, everybody starts looking for someone to blame! And, it seems that the more you try to defend yourself or maybe even your actions, the worse the situation becomes. When you try to seek revenge, the whole scheme blows up in your face! I know! I've tried!

Well, there is something that we all know and that is, Jesus Christ Himself was falsely accused by His own people. On the eve of His crucifixion, Jesus was led from judgement hall to judgement hall to stand before the court, in the face of false accusations (read Luke 23).

What we have to remember is the righteousness of Jesus Christ! The woman who was caught in adultery is an example of our Righteousness in Christ Jesus comes to our rescue. When accusers come to provide false witness against you, think about the woman that was caught in adultery and how Jesus dealt with her accusers (John 8:10). He is the only One who has the authority to judge us! And, as a result, we are "free" in Christ Jesus when we claim Him as our Lord and Savior! He has redeemed us, He has forgiven us and our sins are as far from us as the east is to the west (Psalm 103:12)! So, let us rejoice in our Savior and speak of His righteousness in our praise!

He is my Righteous Judge!

DAY 90

He's Working My Patience

James 1:2, 3— My brethren, count it all joy when you fall into various trials, knowing that the testing of your faith produces patience.

PRAISE DAY 90—There are times in our lives when things just don't or won't go our way. When those times arise, we feel we have to respond. Too many times, our response to those situations is such that the situation becomes worse and not better. Afterwards, we wonder why.

There are also times in our lives when our response to situations it to identify who or what to blame. You want to blame people around you who often times include your spouse and/or your children. You want to blame your co-workers for assignments not being completed on time. You even want to blame traffic when you fail to arrive at a specified appointment in a timely manner. Then, when you are upset because of someone's actions or failure to act, you may be thinking, as we say often, he's working my nerves!

We have to know and remember that situations are neutral. Our response to these situations is what causes them to be positive, negative or remain neutral. Whatever your response, it is your decision! When we fall into circumstances where we feel as if our faith is being tested it may be that God is actually, working on your patience! Instead of asking Him for more patience, praise Him in those situations where your patience is necessary to endure a test!

PRAISE REPORT:

_____

_____

_____

_____

_____

_____

_____

_____

_____

_____

_____

_____

_____

_____

_____

_____

DAY 91

Praise God at Midnight

Psalm 119:62-- **For At midnight I will rise to give thanks to You, Because of Your righteous judgments.**

PRAISE DAY 91—I don't know about you, but for me, the worst times to receive a phone call is between the hours of midnight and 4 in the morning! When the phone rings during those hours, if you are like me, your heart pounds and your mind races! Even though we may be fearful of the news that might be awaiting us on the other end, with shaking hands and nervous anticipation, we snatch the phone off the receiver, or in today's time, grab the cellular phone off the charger.

One of those dark moments came when the phone rang in the early morning hours. The voice on the other end of the line told me that my grandmother, whom I love dearly, was being rushed to the hospital and that the family was being called to begin praying. In obedience, I jumped out of bed, fell to my knees and began crying out to the Lord!

In the midst of my cries, I heard in a still small voice, "Your grandmother is fine. Stop crying and start praising!" Immediately there was a calmness in my spirit. I dried my tear and praised the Lord for my grandmother's recover. And, the Lord did it! She lived for more years after that, for which our family is so grateful. In times of distress, even then, remember His Righteousness and praise Him in your darkest hour.

PRAISE IN DARK TIMES REPORT:

_____

_____

_____

_____

_____

_____

_____

_____

_____

_____

_____

_____

_____

_____

_____

_____

_____

_____

DAY 92

I Sing Because I'm Happy

Psalm 40:3-- For He has put a new song in my mouth—
Praise to our God;
Many will see it and fear,
And will trust in the LORD.

PRAISE DAY 92—"His Eye is on the Sparrow" is a favored hymn written by Civilla D. Martin. The words to the song and its meaning can be linked to the verses of Scripture found in chapter 10 of Matthew's Gospel, beginning with verse 29:

"29 Are not two sparrows sold for a farthing? and one of them shall not fall on the ground without your Father. 30 But the very hairs of your head are all numbered. 31 Fear ye not therefore, ye are of more value than many sparrows." KJV

The comfort to us that is found in these words lies in the fact that everything God created exists at His command. Everything we are or ever hope to be can be found in Him. So, why am I worried about tomorrow when I know if I trust Him, my life is in

His hand? Others are watching to see how Christians respond in trying times. While non-believers may be fearful, we can rest in knowing that God, who cares about the sparrow, also cares about me! Cast your cares on Him today and rejoice in the lightening of your burdens!

SING A NEW SONG!

DAY 93

He's Everywhere I am

Psalm 139:8—If I ascend into heaven, You are there; If I make my bed in hell, behold, You are there.

PRAISE DAY 93—In 1967, Marvin Gaye, along with Tammi Terrell released a single entitled, "Ain't No Mountain High Enough". The lyrics were the original writings of Nick Ashford and Valerie Simpson, aka "Ashford & Simpson". Although their song is about mutual lovers, it constantly reminds me of the verses of Scripture found in Psalm 139. We can find comfort in these words! There is nothing, not even hell itself that can keep us from the Lord!

Even when I have gone astray, if I just call out to Him, cry out to Him, He will reach and grab me! I also am reminded that I must not allow anything or anyone come between my Lord and me. I cannot allow my status in life, my position on the job, the money that I may or may not have, friends, nor family, keep me from the love of God. Praise the Lord because He has never left me nor has He forsaken me. Wherever I go, His is with me!

PRAISE HIM FOR HIS PRESENCE:

DAY 94

I am Content

Philippians 4:11-13— Not that I speak in regard to need, for
I have learned in whatever state I am, to be
content: 12) I know how to be abased, and I know
how to abound. Everywhere and in all things I have
learned both to be full and to be hungry, both to
abound and to suffer need. 13) I can do all things
through Christ who strengthens me.

PRAISE DAY 94—Paul says, in the verses above, that he has learned how to be rich and he has learned how to be poor. He knows how to have everything he needs and how to be in need. Then, he says that Christ strengthens him to go through every state of being.

We are not all rich, neither are we all poor. Many of us are somewhere in between. Paul's verses here tell and teach us that it does not matter what financial state we are in, but it does matter how we respond to our financial situations. From being rich to living from pay check to pay check, to barely making ends meet, to being destitute. Paul says that Christ will enable us to endure those times.

Who would have thought that even when we are rich that we would need Christ to "strengthen" us? Well, we do! There are too many stories where rich individuals were not happy. There are too many stories involving people without wealth who committed crimes to get what they thought would make them happy. In order to be content—meaning without complaint, without sorrow, without guilt—our first priority has to be our relationship with Christ! Praise Him today for whatever state you are in and be content!

CONTENTMENT PRAISE:

_____

_____

_____

_____

_____

_____

_____

_____

_____

_____

_____

_____

_____

_____

DAY 95

Thank Him for Your Job

Psalm 62:12—Also to You, O Lord, belongs mercy;
For You render to each one according to his work.

PRAISE DAY 95—How to get ahead on the job? Treat and work in your position as if you were working for yourself! Better yet, treat and work in your position as if you are working for the Lord!

Ephesians 6:7 (a continuation from verses 5 and 6) reads "…with goodwill doing service, as to the Lord, and not to men." In other words, surrender your service as unto the Lord for He is the One you want to please! When you are working for the Lord, it is classified as surrendered service. When you are working for man, or even in your own business, it is classified as a job! When you only perceive the work you do as a job, then that's all you get because you will have a tendency to expect your reward to come from man. But, when you surrender your labor as service to the Lord, He is the One who will reward you! Now, where do you want your reward to come from?

When you "work" for the Lord, you want to do your very, excellent best. When you focus on pleasing God instead of man, man will have no other recourse but to also be pleased! If you prayed and asked God to bless you with that job, praise Him because He delivered on your prayers! It may not be what you think it should be, but it is where the Lord has blessed you to be! If you find it difficult to praise Him because of the type of work, then bless His Name for your check!

At the end of your day, ask yourself the question, "Is the Lord pleased with my 'work' today?" If you can honestly answer "YES" to this question, give the Lord some praise!

PRAISE THE LORD FOR YOUR SURRENDERED WORK

DAY 96

Cheerful Giver

II Corinthians 9:7--So let each one give as he purposes in his heart, not grudgingly or of necessity; for God loves a cheerful giver.

PRAISE DAY 96—Have you ever received a gift from someone who really did not want to give what they gave to you? Have you ever received a favor from someone who outwardly showed that they really didn't appreciate doing the work for you? How did you feel when those things were done to you? Chances are when they were done to you by someone close to you, the pain was greater. You probably felt, and may have even said, that it would have been better had the person not done anything! You regret their responses so much that the next time you find yourself in need; you don't even want to contact that person!

Think about that for a few seconds and then look at the verse above again. How do you think the Lord feels when we give our offerings, but we do so out of an obligation, or out of necessity, and not out of love for Him? How do you think He feels when we give grudgingly, not really wanting to share our few little dollars that belong to Him in the first place? What about you worrying over your bills, thinking you won't have enough money at the end of your paycheck to pay all of your bills if you give? Don't you hear the Lord saying to you, "Don't you think I'm greater than your paycheck?"

Now that you have praised the Lord for your job and your pay check, it is time for you to bless Him with what He has given you! Without looking at your bills, (pray over them), pray and ask the Lord what He would have you give to Him. Set that aside and PRAISE Him because He promises to meet our needs and more importantly, because He *LOVES* a cheerful giver!

PRAISE THE LORD IN YOUR GIVING!

_____

_____

_____

_____

_____

_____

_____

_____

_____

_____

_____

DAY 97

There is a Blessing in Your Obedience

Malachi 3:10-- Bring all the tithes into the storehouse,
That there may be food in My house,
And try Me now in this,"
Says the LORD of hosts,
"If I will not open for you the windows of heaven
And pour out for you *such* blessing
That *there will* not *be room* enough *to receive it.*

PRAISE DAY 97—Pastors talk about the tithes all the time. The truth of the matter is that the church is the only non-profit organization that relies solely on the donations of its members. Yes, in today's times, pastors and ministers alike solicit funds online. But the bottom line is without the giving of tithes and offerings the church would no longer exist.

For those of you who are already tithing or giving (cheerfully) on a regular basis, you can praise God for the promises He has made to bless you with because of your obedience! 1) He will rebuke the devourer—meaning He will keep robbers, thieves, decay, wear and tear from consuming your personal effects; 2) the fruit of your ground will not be destroyed—whatever you plant (work at) will bring a harvest that the devil will not be able to stop or hinder; 3) The Lord Himself will "open up the windows of heaven and pour out for you such blessing that there will not be room enough to receive it,"—no explanation needed!

If you have not yet begun to tithe or give a fixed amount, I encourage you to pray and ask the Lord to put an amount in your heart that you will commit to out of every paycheck. Then, COMMIT to cheerfully give that amount in obedience to the Lord! As He blesses you and instructs you, increase the amount of your giving! Praise Him now for what you have and for what His is preparing for you!

PRAISE THE LORD IN YOUR OBEDIENCE!

DAY 98

Praise God for Increase

Psalm 115:14-- May the LORD give you increase more and
more,
You and your children.

PRAISE DAY 98—Psalm 115 serves as encouragement to those in the Body of Christ. We are encouraged to glorify God with the understanding that He is the only One who deserves our praise and worship. Unlike idol gods of gold and silver, our God is our "help: and "shield" (verses 9-11). Whereas idol gods have mouths but cannot speak, hands but cannot handle, ears but cannot hear, eyes but cannot hear, (verses verses 4-8), our God is "mindful of us" (verse 12), meaning He has all of the physical capabilities to speak, hear, move, touch and more.

We are therefore encouraged to continue putting our trust of the Lord, our God. In our faithfulness, He promises to bless us, "both small and great" (verse 13) and as our verse above indicates, with this blessing come increase! Just imagine a positive influx in every area of your life! This blessing is for us and our children as well. He has given us this earth to provide us with everything we need. Because of this provision, we can, we should, we will, praise His Name!

Take a few moments and PRAISE THE LORD!

_____

_____

_____

_____

_____

_____

_____

_____

_____

_____

_____

_____

_____

_____

_____

_____

_____

_____

_____

DAY 99

Praise Under Pressure

Malachi 3:3-- He will sit as a refiner and a purifier of silver;
He will purify the sons of Levi,
And purge them as gold and silver,
That they may offer to the LORD
An offering in righteousness.

PRAISE DAY 99—Have you ever gone through something so dark and intense you thought you would melt under the pressure? Something that is internal that you can't share with others? You tell yourself to trust God as you watch others receive blessings. I have been there many times. I was so tired, frustrated and weary. Then, I studied the process that a diamond goes through. It helped me to understand the development God expects when He tells us to be fruitful and multiply. Let me share it with you.

A diamond is highly concentrated carbon. Yes, carbon, one of the most common elements in the world that is essential for humans for even the air we breathe contains carbon. According to science, diamonds form about 100 miles below the Earth's surface, in the molten rock of the Earth's mantle. Here there is just enough pressure and heat to transform carbon into a diamond. In order for a diamond to be created, carbon must be placed under at least

435,113 pounds per square inch (psi) of pressure at a temperature of at least 752 degrees Fahrenheit. If the conditions drop below either of these two points, graphite will be created instead of diamonds.

I must pause here to tell you that God knows just how much heat and pressure we can stand. This heat and pressure enables us to form into a jewel fit for the King of king's use. The Bible states there hath no temptation taken you but such is common to man: but God is faithful, who will not suffer you to be tempted above that ye are able; but will with the temptation also make a way to escape, that ye may be able to bear it (I Co. 10:13). This word tempt comes from the Greek word "peirazo" which means to test, trial or to prove. Hallelujah, God holds all the reins of our testing. He knows what it is that He desires to accomplish, and His plan always works for our good, to give us a hope and a future!

Contributed by Minister Bernita Taylor

Therefore, even under pressure, we should, we must, Praise Him!

PRAISE UNDER PRESSURE REPORT:

_____

_____

_____

_____

_____

_____

_____

_____

_____

_____

_____

_____

_____

_____

_____

_____

_____

DAY 100

Praise Him for Sunshine and Rain

Psalm 68:9-- You, O God, sent a plentiful rain,
Whereby You confirmed Your inheritance,
When it was weary.

PRAISE DAY 18—In 1995 my family and I moved to Southeast Texas. Shortly after the move, I experienced a sudden torrential thunder storm and rain that I had never experienced before. Thunder was so loud and the lightening was so bright and frequent that I was unable to sleep. Whenever I find myself in this type of situation, generally, I pray. While I was praying, the still small voice spoke to me and I was instructed to "stand on the front porch".

In obedience, I opened the front door and stepped out onto the porch. The rains was still coming down, the thunder was still roaring and lightening danced vigorously across the sky. For a moment, I stood there, in fear and I was trembling every time a clap of thunder boomed in the atmosphere. Again, the still small Voice spoke to me saying, "I am there; in the storm and rain!"

This time, when I looked up into the sky, I realize that the lightening, which is essentially fire, was coexisting with the rain, which is essentially water! I was relieved with amazement! Only our God can make fire and water exist at the same time, in the same space! With that revelation, I was reminded of our Scripture found in Psalm 69:9! Too many times, we only want to praise the Lord during our times of blessings and plenty, you know, our "sunshiny days". But, we have to understand that He reminds us of His promises every time it rains! He has never failed me! He will not fail you. So the next time it "rains" in your life, know that God is STILL with you! Praise Him in your sunshine times and in your stormy weather times! He is faithful!

PRAISE THE LORD FOR SUNSHINE AND RAIN

_____

_____

_____

_____

_____

_____

_____

_____

_____

_____

_____

_____

_____

DAY 101

Praise While Waiting

Psalm 27:14 — Wait on the LORD;
Be of good courage,
And He shall strengthen your heart;
Wait, I say, on the LORD!

PRAISE DAY 101—In a brief exposition of the verse above, we realize that "wait" means to look for; expect eagerly; to await. The word "strong" means powerful and mighty; to be strengthened. And, the word "courage" means to be of good cheer. To be of good cheer means, even as one sits, waiting on a command, not knowing if or when it will happen. It also tells me to expect eagerly as I wait for it to happen. Waiting allows one to sit for a while with hope, and anticipation. Also, the waiting allows one's heart to become strong and courageous.

This is how I perceive Psalm 27:14. I didn't always wait for God's timing or answer. Sometimes I went ahead of God, trying to solve it myself. In 2001, my world was turned upside down when my spouse passed away. I was a stay at home mom. My deceased spouse was self-employed so all monetary fund's stopped. The month in which he died I received a letter from IRS stated that we will not be getting a refund check.

Now talking about timing being all wrong! How will I and my children be able to survive? When you are going through something, one always turns back to the problem solver. That is Jesus. I began to meditate on Psalm 27:14. I didn't know when it would happen but I knew that I had to wait on God's timing. It wasn't a request; it was a command. After four weeks I received a refund check in the mail, from the IRS deciding to return the refund check. You might say it was the IRS but I know it was God telling me to wait on Him. Psalm 34:1 says "I will bless the Lord at all times: His praise shall continually be in my mouth." LESSON: God has a time to deliver and bless you; wait for it in faith. Hallelujah!

Contributed by Roberta Sinclair

PRAISE THE LORD AS YOU ARE WAITING!

_____

_____

_____

_____

_____

_____

_____

_____

_____

DAY 102
Give Thanks for He is Good

Psalm 136:— O give thanks unto the Lord; for he is good.

PRAISE DAY 102— This is my favorite Psalm. Going through many changes in my adult life that I never thought I would experience has brought me closer to the Lord. I always imagined that I would grow up like the movies with the husband and two children with the house and white picket fence. And, let's not forget the dog and cat! However, the older I became I began realizing that I was not going to have children of my own. After praying and praying for children of my own, I came to accept that this is not what God has in store for me.

God blessed me with a man who had two children. We have these two children, a son and daughter, who look just like a "mini me"! Having two beautiful children who many believe are my own biological children, based on the way they look and act, I could not have asked for a greater blessing. I am still being blessed with my husband of 15 years. Our daughter is attending Yale, studying ministry. And, our son is in management. I am truly blessed! So, yes, I give thanks unto the Lord; for He is good!

Submitted by Kim Dromgoole

There are times in our lives when things just don't seem right. We pray for people, places and things that don't seem to come to fruition. Nevertheless, we understand that God's ways are not our ways, neither are His thoughts like ours! Whatever we are going through or have gone through, it is for our best interest, if we truly belong to Him and our lives are in His hands! So, rejoice and give God thanks! It may seem like a setback right now, but in reality it is a set up, orchestrated by God!

THANKFUL FOR WHAT I HAVE!

_____

_____

_____

_____

_____

_____

_____

_____

_____

_____

_____

_____

_____

DAY 103
But God!

Psalm 3:3—But You, O LORD, *are* a shield for me,
My glory and the One who lifts up my head.

PRAISE DAY 103—In this Psalm, David starts out writing about the number of enemies that have increased in his life. He further says that those who are against him, declare that God is no longer with him, in essence, because if He was, He wouldn't allow all of those enemies to rise up against David (Psalm 3:1, 2). How often do you feel as if your enemies or trouble is all around you? When was the last time you felt you were drowning in defeat? When was the last time your pillow was damp from your tears that were shed during the wee hours of the night?

Our peace and comfort are found in verse 3 of this particular Psalm, where David writes, "But You, O Lord, are a shield for me. My glory and the One who lifts up my head." Because we are in Christ, there is always a "but" in the middle of our situation! You may be experiencing trouble on your job, BUT GOD is still with you! No matter how many enemies come your way, know that God is still God and He cares for you. He is our shield of protection in those situations. When you are feeling some kind of way, just shout out in praise, BUT GOD!

Make a list of all of your "but God" situations! For example, "I may be sick in my body, BUT GOD said by His stripes, I am healed". I may be lacking today, BUT GOD said He would supply all of my needs according to His riches."

BUT GOD!

_____

_____

_____

_____

_____

_____

_____

_____

_____

_____

_____

_____

_____

_____

_____

_____

DAY 104

God Fills My Cup

Psalm 16:5-- **For O LORD,** *You are* **the portion
of my** inheritance and **my cup;**
You maintain **my** lot.

PRAISE DAY 18—David talks about the people who
would follow God but were putting their trust in idols.
He said that their sorrows were multiplied because of
their desire to follow other gods. David understood that those who
served other gods found many sorrows in life.

David knew that in dedicating his life and living for God,
was not an easy one. There were many hardships he had to endure
because he remained faithful to God. He also knew that life lived
after another god would bring even more sorrow and suffering.
Even today, Christians have to realize that a life without Christ is a
life full of pain, suffering and sorrow. I may go through difficult
times, and we all do, but when those times come in my life, I know
that I am not alone!

David reminds us that the Lord is our portion of our
inheritance and He continually fills my cup. He maintains my
inheritance, meaning He holds and keeps my eternal inheritance
that no one can take from me. With that in mind, I can praise Him!

Lord God, I praise You this day, with all my heart! You fill my cup, Father! You cause my cup to overflow with Your blessings. You provide everything I need every day, to help me grow spiritually. I thank you for revealing Yourself to me and for revealing who I am in You! You are my everlasting inheritance You are the light in my life and my salvation! Praise Your holy Name!

Contributed by Ethel "Mother" Ellis

THANK GOD FOR FULLNESS

_____

_____

_____

_____

_____

_____

_____

_____

_____

_____

_____

_____

_____

_____

DAY 105
He is My Strong Tower

Proverbs 18:10--The name of the LORD is a strong tower; the righteous run into it and are safe.

PRAISE DAY 105—With so many terrorist attacks and threats of terrorist attacks around the world, many people are wondering just how safe are we. We all want to feel safe and secure. Terrorist use this very desire for safety to strike fear in our hearts and cause us to panic and be shaken. Bullies also use these same tactics which causes fear in some of our neighborhoods and schools. Even childcare facilities and their ability to provide a safe environment for our children are genuine concerns today. How do we protect ourselves, our loved one, and our communities? Does true safety and security lie within our local or national armed forces? These, too, are being questioned today. Does it revolve around our personal security systems and alarms? What about our careers, education, societal positions or finances? I think we can all agree that none of these can truly provide us a solid foundation on which to stand. We must look beyond this world to find true security.

Of the fifty references to towers in the Holy Scriptures, all but one, the Tower of Babel, describe towers as belonging to a fortress. The tower of Babel stood as a symbol of humanity striving to go beyond the limits of God. In the bible, four types of towers were built to provide some sort of safety and protection from enemies.

As we can see, from ancient days until today, no man has been able to establish a surety of safety except the One who came into this world as the Son of God. He is the only One to which we can run to in this life and in preparation for the afterlife and find safety. No matter what challenges you are facing today, you have a Strong Tower to which you can run into and find safety. Let us take the time to write a thank you note to the One who is able to keep us and present us faultless.

Contributed by Minister Bernita Taylor

MY STRONG TOWER:

_____

_____

_____

_____

_____

_____

_____

_____

_____

_____

DAY 106

Praise Him for Your Spouse

Ephesians 5:33-- **Nevertheless let each one of you in particular so love his own wife as himself, and let the wife see that she respects her husband.**

PRAISE **DAY 18**—Marriage is a choice!* The man decides he wants to be a husband and possibly a father. When he makes up in his mind that this is the life he chooses, it is then he prepares to ask someone, a woman to marry him. The woman makes a conscious decision to either accept or reject his proposal.

Before either of you—the man or the woman—make the choice to engage in this lifelong commitment to one another, it is wise and necessary that you pray! Pray before you enter into marriage so that you will be able to *praise* after the vows are spoken for years to come. Firstly, pray that this spouse is the one that God has ordained for you. Pray and ask the Lord to guide you before you make and/or accept the proposal. During the marriage, continually pray that the Lord remain first so that love and respect will remain.

(*In countries where young girls are sold into a marriage, this is not a marriage! It is another form of sexual slavery. There are many organizations today that work to end this type of forced servanthood. In the USA, you can contact the **National Human Trafficking Resource Center at 1 (888) 373-7888** for more information.).

If you are already married, take a few moments to list the things about your spouse that you love, respect and appreciate. If you are still waiting, list the characteristics you are searching for in a spouse (you have to live up to your list first!). If your spouse has gone on before you, take time to praise God for the life you had together, list and cherish those things about your spouse that you treasure, even today.

GOD, I LOVE MY SPOUSE!

_____

_____

_____

_____

_____

_____

_____

_____

_____

_____

_____

DAY 107

Praise Him for Your Children

Matthew 19:13-- Then were there brought unto him little children, that he should put his hands on them, and pray: and the disciples rebuked them.

PRAISE DAY 107—Children are a gift from God! Psalm 127:3 reads, "Behold, children *are* a heritage from the LORD, The fruit of the womb *is* a reward." And, if you have ever studied the human life cycle, you would understand why conception is called a "miracle"! There are so many reasons why a woman would not or could not get pregnant, so when it happens, it is a gift that can only come from God!

Children are our heritage! They are our future! They are our next generation resources. They will be the ones who will take care of us when we can no longer take care of ourselves. However, they will only do for us what we do for them and only then, if we train them now to do so! Not only are we to train them up in the way they should go (Proverbs 22:6; this is God's promise), but we must pray for them!

If you don't have any children, praise God for the children you plan to have in your future! If you are past the years of child bearing, then pray for the children in your neighborhood. Every

---

child you see today, praise God for that child, pray for that child's future, pray that the child has a real relationship with Jesus Christ and that he/she will become everything that God has created them to be!

PRAYING AND PRAISING GOD FOR THESE CHILDREN:

_____

_____

_____

_____

_____

_____

_____

_____

_____

_____

_____

_____

_____

_____

_____

_____

_____

DAY 108

Praise Him for Your Friends and Family

Proverbs 18:24-- A man who has friends must himself be friendly, But there is a friend who sticks closer than a brother.

PRAISE DAY 108—Ours is a big family! My mother gave birth to 8 children and we all have children. Now, our children have their children and even some have their own grandchildren! Every family reunion we are introduced to more and more children! We also have included other people's children into our family. We all have at one point or another, taken in someone who was in need of a family. I hear other people, all the time, call me "grandma", "Mother" or even "mom". It does my heart good to know that other people care about me and I care about them as if we are family.

The truth of the matter is, if we are in Christ Jesus, we *are* family! If we all could just take a hold of that idea and treat each other like family, we could change the world! Let us love one another today and forever, the way Jesus intended. Show yourself friendly, and be a friend. Remember, Jesus is the greatest friend we have ever had and He is our example.

Contributed by Ethel "Mother" Ellis

PRAISE GOD FOR FAMILY AND FRIENDS

DAY 109

Be a Family that Praises Together

Joshua 24:15-- "And if it seems evil to you to serve the LORD, choose for yourselves this day whom you will serve, whether the gods which your fathers served that were on the other side of the River, or the gods of the Amorites, in whose land you dwell. But as for me and my house, we will serve the LORD."

PRAISE DAY 109—Worshipping together as a family has always been part of our lives. From the time I was a little girl, up into my present, we have always made sure to include worship in our family. It is the standard as well as the rule in our family. Not only is prayer important in the family unit, but also worship and praise of our Lord should be included.

Prayer and praising God together is a very important part of family unity and should be practiced individually, together as family heads, and together as a family. Satan knows the power of praise, worship and the power in unity. Therefore, he will do everything he can in order to keep you, your spouse and your family from praying, worshipping and praising God together.

Be encouraged this week to engage your family in a "sing-along" of praise and worship songs! Get together your favorite Christian and/or Gospel songs and praise the Lord together as a family. You may even want to start out with a family prayer, asking each member to share their prayer requests, then close out with praise! If you don't have family close, then invite or gather up some friends, the next time you have a gathering at your home, and praise the Lord together!

Write down the family prayer requests.

FAMILY PRAYER AND PRAISE DAY

_____

_____

_____

_____

_____

_____

_____

_____

_____

_____

_____

_____

_____

_____

_____

DAY 110

Strength for the Weary

Isaiah 40:31 -- But those who wait on the LORD
Shall renew their strength;
They shall mount up with wings like eagles,
They shall run and not be weary,
They shall walk and not faint.

PRAISE DAY 110— In these verses of Scripture, Isaiah 40:27-31, Israel is in captivity for disobedience and feel as though they have dug a ditch so deep for themselves and angered God to a point of no return or redemption. When I was a young teenager, I became pregnant. I was happy, afraid, ashamed and disgraced. I was happy because I thought I would finally have someone to love me....all the other feeling are obvious. However, I was taken to get an abortion. I sat in that clinic for hours, just sobbing. I was so alone. I had tried to commit suicide by engulfing all the pills in the medicine cabinet, yet, there I was sitting in the clinic alone, confused and sobbing.

I eventually had the abortion that day. I hemorrhaged the rest of that day. It was not until I was taken to the doctor for a checkup, that I discovered I should have died from the loss of so much blood. It wasn't until years later that I realized that loss of blood was from the pills that I had taken the night before.

However, at that young age, I did not know the forgiveness of God. I thought He will never love me now. See, I grew up in church. My grandfather gave me a bible when I was 10 years old. I read it and love it and the LORD. I read about the nations who had sacrificed their children to idols. I felt that I had sacrificed my children in order to save my own life. I thought God will never love and accept me now......

After returning to God in my twenties, one day I was contemplating that fact that He was calling me to preach. I did not understand how He could call me to such a great assignment. I was singing in the choir and teaching the youth in Sunday school. Along with serving as a youth and choir director, I had even spoken on a few occasions. However, the call to preach hit me like a ton of bricks. I had to first get over the fact that I was a woman, but now the constant reminder of all the blood...the blood flowing from me......the blood of my lost child....

I cried out to God; LORD don't You remember the blood. How could You call me to preach. I'm so unworthy. I'm so unclean. And in the midst of my sobbing I heard Him say. No, I do not remember the blood....my heart sank lower. How could the All-Knowing, All-wise God not remember the blood. Then, I heard Him say but My Son's blood was more powerful than your child's blood and it washed your child's blood away. So, you see I do not remember...Now, go and preach My gospel to the lost, the broken-hearted, the captive and the destitute.

Yes, I fell....but it was at His feet. At His feet, He giveth power to the faint and to them that have not might He increases strength. His love and His mercy gave me power beyond my limitations and strength that overcomes doubts and fears. He renewed my strength to serve Him unconditionally. I felt like I had wings as eagles. I am able to run and not be weary and to walk and not faint. Our purpose for living is found only in the Almighty who has to power to keep us from falling and cause us to stand. Let past issues go today. Write them out; then, release them to God, giving Him praise, that He might strengthen you.

Contributed by Minister Bernita Taylor

PRAISE GOD FOR STRENGTH

_____

_____

_____

_____

_____

_____

_____

_____

_____

_____

_____

_____

D'AY 111

He is My Counselor

Psalm 16:7— I will bless the LORD who has given me counsel; My heart also instructs me in the night seasons.

PRAISE DAY 111—It is in our desperate times that we feel the need for good counsel the most. More often than not, we tend to seek out those who are closest to us for the counsel that we so urgently. Even more, those who are closest to us give us advice and try to influence us based on their own experiences and/or their own needs. Sometimes, our friends advise us based on their own agendas.

For the most part, the Word of God is full of His advice and He always provides us with good counsel! Whatever your counseling needs are, you can find a Word from the Lord! There are subjects regarding marriage, children, finances, holy living and more. As you are reading, seeking His guidance, pray for His direction, understanding and wisdom! You can also pray that He directs you to the right person to talk to about your issue, if further, earthly counsel is needed! Yes, you can do that!

After all is said and done, don't forget to praise His for His counsel. He speaks to our hearts and spirits, if only we would listen!

PRAISE GOD FOR HIS WISE COUNSEL:

DAY 112

He's Everything I Need and More

Philippians 4:19-- And my God shall supply all your need according to His riches in glory by Christ Jesus.

PRAISE DAY 18—Everything we need, our God promises to supply! However, don't get lost in the truth of that statement! God promises to supply our needs, but the way He may choose to supply them may not be what we thought or in a manner to our liking. For example, you may be praying for $1 (just an example). Don't get upset if that dollar comes in the form of ten dimes, or four quarters, or twenty nickels! What is it came to you in the form of one hundred pennies? Each one of these is the $1 that you have prayed for and you are in need of. We might miss out on our blessing is someone offers us something, and because of our pride, we refuse to accept it!

Matthew 6:8b tells us, "...For your Father knows the things you have need of before you ask Him". If you have children, you might understand this concept even more. We know that we have to feed our children. We are obligated to do that. But, how many times have you prepared the meal and the child refused to or fussed about eating it because it wasn't want they wanted? How did that make you feel? God provides us with what we need. It is ours to accept or reject what He has given! The house may not be the house you want, but it is a house! The neighborhood may not be the one you want but it may be the one where God wants to use you! The same thing goes for the job, the car, the spouse, the children and more, all the way down to the small things like the shoes on your feet and the clothes on your back. Today, instead of complaining about what you want, praise God for what you already have!

PRAISE GOD FOR FULFILLING MY NEEDS:

_____

_____

_____

_____

_____

_____

_____

_____

_____

_____

_____

_____

_____

_____

DAY 113

The Great I AM

Psalm 81:10-- For I am the LORD your God,
Who brought you out of the land of Egypt;
Open your mouth wide, and I will fill it.

PRAISE DAY 113—When reading the Book of Exodus you will learn that the children of Israel had to constantly be reminded of who God is. Even with all of the miracles He performed for them, the children of Israel still doubted and at times even rebelled! Throughout their travels in the desert, their leader Moses, had to remind them that God is the *One* who delivered them from Egypt. He fed the bread from heaven, sent quail for meat, brought water from a rock and led them through the Red Sea on dry ground! And, to top it off, God caused Pharaoh's army to drown in the same sea!

When Moses first met with and spoke to God, the Lord identified Himself as "I AM". This Name is so sufficient because any other name would not be *big* enough! That Name, "I AM", refers to a constant state of being; no beginning and no ending. Eternal, everlasting, all existing, always and forever! We can praise our GREAT I AM, because He still **IS**! As Revelation 1:8 declares, our God is, "I am Alpha and Omega, the beginning and the ending, says the Lord, which is, and which was, and which is to come, the Almighty." There is no ending in Him!

PRAISE THE GREAT *I AM*:

_____

_____

_____

_____

_____

_____

_____

_____

_____

_____

_____

_____

_____

_____

_____

_____

_____

_____

_____

DAY 114

Come, Let Us Worship Him

Psalm 99:9-- Exalt the LORD our God,
And worship at His holy hill;
For the LORD our God *is* holy.

PRAISE DAY 114—One of my favorite hymns is one that is generally reserved for Christmas time. It is "Oh, Come, All Ye Faithful", which was originally written in Latin by Adeste Fideles. According to online resources, this hymn has also been attributed to various authors, including John Francis Wade (1711–1786), with the earliest copies of the hymn all bearing his signature, John Reading (1645–1692) and King John IV of Portugal (1604–1656.

It doesn't really matter to me who wrote it, I'm just glad that it was written! It is so simple yet so rich and full. If you know the song, pause right here and just sing it for a moment! (pause) How do you feel now? How does that compare to how you were feeling before you sang the song? Did you want to close your eyes and lift up your hands in worship? You would if you are a true worshipper!

Today, set aside some time to worship our Lord and Savior! For He alone is worthy! For He has sanctified me, with His blood

He has saved me, with His power He has raised me! Christ is the Lord of my life! I cannot live without Him! What other verses can you make up? Write them down and include them in your singing.

PRAISE REPORT:

_____

_____

_____

_____

_____

_____

_____

_____

_____

_____

_____

_____

_____

_____

_____

DAY 115

He is My Promise Keeper

Psalm 105:42-- For He remembered His holy **promise**, *And* Abraham His servant.

PRAISE DAY 115—There are times when we might be discouraged. It is the way of life. Looking at Psalm 105 in its entirety, the writer lists the things that the Israelites endured, even after receiving God's promise to take them to a land flowing with milk and honey (Exodus 3:8). For generations, the people of God had to go through hardships like famine, slavery, and travel through the desert with no water. God kept them, protected them, fed them, and provided them with water and manna from heaven. When they wanted meat, He gave them quail. He kept them because of His promise to Abraham so many years before.

When we examine all that they suffered and all that God did for them, it gives us reason to praise God! We are living the promise! The promise of joy, peace, the promise of salvation, the promise of eternity and so much more, God has and still is providing to us. He still blesses us, protects us and keeps us, because of His promise. He is our promise keeper!

Rejoice today, because of His promises! Read through the

"red" words in the New Testament and locate the promises that have been provided to us. Rejoice! Because, just as God has kept His promise to bring the children of Israel to the land of Canaan, He keeps His promises to us! Write down the promises that mean the most to you and give God praise!

PROMISE KEEPER PRAISE REPORT:

_____

_____

_____

_____

_____

_____

_____

_____

_____

_____

_____

_____

_____

_____

_____

_____

DAY 116

Lover of My Soul

Isaiah 38:17-- Behold, for peace I had great bitterness: but
thou hast in love to my soul delivered it from the
pit of corruption: for thou hast cast all my sins
behind thy back. (KJV)

PRAISE DAY 116—A young man entered my office and said he really needed to speak to me. I quickly noticed that he was covered with satanic tattoos and that he had a large satanic goat tattooed on his chest. When I asked him why he was covered in those tattoos, he said, "It's because I'm a devil worshiper." To which I replied, "Well, I'm a JESUS Worshiper. I'm going to let you talk and then I'm going to talk." After sharing conversation for a while, I asked him, "So, why do you worship the devil?"

Him: Because I'm an evil person. I know that repenting for me is useless because I don't want to change.

Me: So, why do you want to talk to me?

Him: Because I've been hearing about you and I believe you can help me.

Me: Did you sell your soul to the devil?

Him: Yes I did.

Me: You know you can't believe in the devil without believing in

God.

Him: Yes, I know.

Me: and you know what happens to him in the end.

Him: Yes, he loses.

Me: Well, let me set you free right now. You can't sell what does not belong to you.

Him: What???

Me: Your soul--you can't sell it because it does not belong to you. It belongs to God!

Him: Wow! I didn't know that!

After much more conversation, the young man said, "You have said some things to me that have made more sense than anything anyone else has said when they were trying to get me to convert back to Christianity. You have changed my life!"

Me: Amen! Come back any time!

The Lord is the lover and keeper of our souls! He does not want any of us to miss out on the opportunity to be with Him in eternity! No matter where you are in your life, as long as there is breath in your body, you can give your life and your soul to Him! It is His anyway! Now, give God praise for those on your prayer list who still have the opportunity to be saved!

PRAISE REPORT:

_____

_____

_____

_____

_____

_____

_____

_____

_____

_____

_____

_____

_____

_____

_____

_____

_____

_____

_____

_____

_____

DAY 117

I Will Not Worry

Philippians 4:9—Be careful for nothing; but in everything by prayer and supplication with thanksgiving let your requests be made known unto God.

PRAISE DAY 117—We all have struggles. As the saying goes, "you are either in a storm, just coming out of a storm or about ready to enter into a storm". Stormy days come in all shapes and fashions. We all have them! We can look back in the Word of God and see that even the most dedicated, most holy, most faithful people in the Bible also had their stormy days!

When I minister to non-believers who think Christians should never have a problem, I let them know that we do, however, the thing that separates me from them is the way I respond when I am in a difficult situation and that fact that I can pray, expecting God to do something, even if that "something" is just comforting me while I am going through! God may not always take me out of the storm, but He did promise to be with me in it (Matthew 28:20)! Because I know He is always with me, I don't worry! Whenever I feel myself "slipping" into a slump or into a pity party, I turn up the praise! I know that God is working on my concerns!

Write down the things you are concerned and anxious about. Once you have written them down, believe that the Lords has them in His hands! Now, let go of them and praise God. If you don't have any concerns right now, that's even more reason to Praise the Lord!

PRAISE REPORT:

_____

_____

_____

_____

_____

_____

_____

_____

_____

_____

_____

_____

_____

_____

_____

_____

DAY 118

Take it to Jesus

Matthew 9:2-- And, behold, they brought to him a man sick of the palsy, lying on a bed: and Jesus seeing their faith said unto the sick of the palsy; Son, be of good cheer; thy sins be forgiven thee.

PRAISE DAY 118—Do you have an issue that you just can't resolve? Are you worried about something that you cannot handle alone? In this verse, there were some men who brought this sick man to Jesus. These men are identified by Jesus as having faith. They had faith enough to believe that Jesus would heal the man if only they could get him to Jesus. Christ is ready and willing to relieve us of what troubles us! But, we have to have faith enough to bring it to Him and release our matters into His capable hands.

Are you lying in bed at night, tossing and turning because of trouble in your life? Well, ponder on this: In order to get a good night's sleep, you have to empty yourself of everything that would cause you to toss and turn during the night, causing you to lose sleep! Before you go to sleep tonight, I admonish you to play some worship type music, the kind of music that makes you want to be closer to Christ. As the music is play, bow down before the Lord and "empty" your soul out to Him! Everything that you have on your mind, release it to Him. The best way to get a good night's sleep is to go to be "empty"! That way, in the morning, you will wake up empty and as you praise God for another day, He will be able to "fill" you with His glory!

PRAISE REPORT:

_____

_____

_____

_____

_____

_____

_____

_____

_____

_____

_____

_____

_____

_____

_____

_____

_____

DAY 119

Blessings Overtake You

Deuteronomy 28:2-- "And all these blessings shall come upon you and overtake you, because you obey the voice of the LORD your God:

PRAISE DAY 119—It is so easy for Christians to remember their favorite promises that are written in the Word of God. However, there are times that the prerequisites are faint or vague memories in our minds. Even reading the verse above, we quickly read that ALL of the BLESSINGS shall come upon [US] and overtake [US]! But, what we have to be most mindful of is the command for obedience that will cause the blessing to manifest! When we obey, God will bless!

It is the same way with us and our children, or at least it should be! When our children are obedient, we bless them. Sometimes we bless them with more than what they have asked for simply because we love them. God does the same for us, but if you really, really want a blessing that overtakes you, we have to be obedient to the voice of the Lord. His voice is in His Word!

Blessings that overtake you would be as if you are standing on the sea shore with your back to the sea. Then, when you least expect it, a huge wave comes up behind your and drenches you!

You become so wet that everybody knows it! You are so wet that everyone you touch also gets wet. Blessings that overtake you will be so much that you become living proof of God's goodness and a living example of His blessings upon His people! When the Lord blesses you to this magnitude, He expects others to benefit from you being blessed also! Now, shout and give God praise for your obedience and the anticipation of His blessing!

PRAISE REPORT:

_____

_____

_____

_____

_____

_____

_____

_____

_____

_____

_____

_____

_____

_____

DAY 120

When I'm Overwhelmed

Psalm 143:8-- Cause me to hear Your lovingkindness in the
morning,
For in You do I trust;
Cause me to know the way in which I should walk,
For I lift up my soul to You.

PRAISE DAY 120—Being overwhelmed is like being in the middle of the ocean, on a row boat, at night time, by yourself, with sharks swimming around and waves tossing you back and forth. Close your eyes for a moment and envision that picture. How did that make you feel?

There are times when we feel that anxiety when things happen in our lives, back to back. For example, you have a bad day at work, you failed to complete an assignment, your boss yells at you, you leave the job to find you have a flat tire; you open the trunk of your car and see that your spare is also flat. You finally get the tire fixed after hours have passed. You get home and find your electricity has been turned off, not because you didn't pay the bill, but because you forgot to mail the check (or as in today's times, you failed to push the "SUBMIT" button when you did it online). Then you call the electric company and they tell you that your energy will not be restored until the next work day which is Monday. Oh, and all of this happens on a Thursday and the following Friday is a holiday! Feeling overwhelmed? Ever had a day like that?

In this Psalm, David is in a state of being overwhelmed! He cries out to God, asking Him to remind David of His loving kindness. He also asks the Lord to guide his footsteps. David realizes that his hope is in continuing to trust God! We too can continue to trust in the Lord when it seems as if everything in our lives is falling apart! When you feel overwhelmed, pray and then Praise! Below, write down a time when you felt overwhelmed. Know that if the Lord brought you through that time (I know He did because you are able to read this passage today), surely He will bring you out the next time!

PRAISE REPORT:

_____

_____

_____

_____

_____

_____

_____

_____

_____

DAY 121

He Strengthens Me

Philippians 4:13-- I can do all things through Christ who strengthens me.

PRAISE DAY 121—In his letter to the Philippians, Paul writes, "I know how to be abased, and I know how to abound. Everywhere and in all things I have learned both to be full and to be hungry, both to abound and to suffer need. I can do all things through Christ who strengthens me," (Philippians 4:12, 13).

Paul says that he has been rich and he has been poor. He indicates he has been full and he has been hungry. He also states the he has lived a life that was full and plentiful as well as a time in his life where he has been in need. He has even had to suffer in prison where he was beaten and bound with chains. Then Paul declared that in each of those situations, it is Christ who has given him strength during each of those times.

We are no different than Paul. We will and do have our good times and bad, our full times and times when we are in need or want. We have times when things are going well and times when it seems as if everything is falling to pieces. We have to be like Paul and realize where our strength comes from! We need the strength that Christ provides in poor times as well as rich or good times! We need Him because we don't want our wealth and prosperity to get in the way of our relationship with Christ! The strength Paul is referring to is not something physical, but spiritual! We need a "right spirit" to live a Christ-like life regardless of our situation! Give God praise for the strength we have on a daily basis that is in Christ Jesus!

PRAISE REPORT:

_____

_____

_____

_____

_____

_____

_____

_____

_____

_____

_____

_____

_____

_____

DAY 122

All Things are Possible

Mark 9:23—Jesus said to him, "If you can believe, all things are possible to him who believes."

PRAISE DAY 122—"The wealthiest place on earth is the graveyard because it is full of people with unfulfilled dreams!" one of my college professor stated during his course introduction. He was trying to encourage the students in his class to not only make it through the course, but also to make it through college to graduation. And, he encouraged us to dream big in the pursuit of our careers and the goals we have set for our lives.

I am a firm believer in the "seed" principle. In Genesis 1:11, God said that every seed will bring forth fruit according to its seed. In other words, everything that a full grown oak tree needed to reach its full potential was already in the seed!

In Genesis 3:15 and again in 4:25, God indicated that we are also "seeds"! Therefore, I believe everything we need to reach our full potential is already in us, from the day God made us. In Exodus 35:35, we read that God "filled them with skill to do all manner of work…"! If He did it in Genesis and in Exodus, He is still doing it today!

So, what keeps us from reaching our goals? Thoughts of

failure? Fear? Uncertainty? Our verse of Scripture today serves as a reminder to us that if we believe, then all things are possible! What would you do if money and time was not an object? What dreams do you have that you have not accomplished yet? Do you still want to pursue that dream? Be encouraged! Pursuit it through prayer, asking God for His wisdom and direction! And, praise your way to your success! If you have already accomplished everything you believe God has for you, that's even more reason to praise Him!

WRITE YOUR DREAMS OR ACCOMPLISHMENTS:

_____

_____

_____

_____

_____

_____

_____

_____

_____

_____

_____

_____

_____

_____

DAY 123
I Will Not Faint

PRAISE DAY 123—The King James Version of this verse reads, "And let us not be weary in well doing: for in due season we shall reap, if we <u>faint</u> not." You can probably remember a time or two where you have done something "good" for someone and your good deed either went unnoticed or unappreciated. There have even been times when my good deeds have been vehemently rejected! I have been told, "I didn't ask you to do that! You just messed it up! That's not how I wanted that done!" Or even, "Why are you messing with my stuff?" It is at those times when I feel weary and want to cry. I feel as if my good deed was not appreciated. Then, I remember this verse.

What we also have to remember is; God is not going to hold us responsible for how other people treat us, but He will hold us responsible for how we treat them! So, even when others reject what I have selflessly given or done, I know that God is still pleased with me! When the time comes, either on this side or in Glory, I will be rewarded; I will reap the benefits that come from doing "good"!

Take extra precaution today to do "good"! Do good works for someone and even for yourself, knowing that when your time comes, you will reap what you have sown!

Give God a "good" praise!

PRAISE REPORT:

_____

_____

_____

_____

_____

_____

_____

_____

_____

_____

_____

_____

_____

_____

_____

_____

DAY 124

Facing My Giants

I Samuel 17:37—Moreover David said, "The LORD, who delivered me from the paw of the lion and from the paw of the bear, He will deliver me from the hand of this Philistine." And Saul said to David, "Go, and the LORD be with you!"

PRAISE DAY 124—There are all kinds of giants in our lives! There is competition on the job. There are supervisors who are out to destroy you. There are financial giants, medical and disease giants, past and present giants and more.

Too many times we try to fight our giant situations the same way that other people did. We take the advice of our friends and our family, without asking God for or seeking His Word for advice. Know that the destruction of your giants is not contingent upon your size! It is not even contingent upon your own ability! It is, however, contingent upon your faith to face the giant, realize that he is there and then realize that it is not the giant that you are fighting, but it is the giant who is fighting against the JESUS in you!

There are other times when we want and allow others to fight our battles for us. In David's situation, the battle actually belonged to King Saul! But, because he was fearful (along with the other Israelites who were afraid to fight), Saul did not want to face his giant. When Saul allowed David to fight for him, David not only received the victory, but he received the blessing! How many of your blessings have you given away simply because you did not want to face the giant complications in your life? In these situations, what I have come to realize is this: giant inconveniences are often a prelude or set up for a giant opportunity that requires work!

What "giant" obstacles have you had in your life or that you currently face? Profess that you are triumphant! Write them down and praise God for your victory over them!

PRAISE REPORT:

_____

_____

_____

_____

_____

_____

_____

_____

_____

_____

DAY 125

God Everlasting

Psalm 90:2-- **Before the mountains were brought forth,
Or ever You had formed the earth and the world,
Even from everlasting to everlasting, You *are* God.**

PRAISE DAY 125—"In the beginning, God"! These are the first words in the Bible. Our God is the only deity that has done things that other gods have not been able to claim. When I read where God said, "Let there be light," and BOOM! There was light! I get so excited! Then I read that God is LIGHT! He shows up in our darkest hours to shed light on our situation. When I see my condition in His light, the fear of what I may be going through disappears, the same way darkness disappears when a light is turned on in a dark room.

Time after time God identifies Himself as Everlasting. He is the Alpha and Omega, the First and the Last, the Beginning and the End! Everything in between, He is, He was, and His is to come. That means He is past, He is present and He is future! Now who wouldn't serve a God like that?

Praises be to our Everlasting Lord!

PRAISE REPORT:

_____

_____

_____

_____

_____

_____

_____

_____

_____

_____

_____

_____

_____

_____

_____

_____

_____

_____

DAY 126

He is My Strong Refuge

Psalm 71:7, 8-- I am as a wonder unto many; but thou [art] my strong refuge. 8 Let my mouth be filled [with] thy praise [and with] thy honour all the day.(KJV)

PRAISE DAY 126—When I think about this Psalm, I am reminded of this song: "My Soul Loves Jesus" (second verse)

He's a wonder in my soul

He's a wonder in my soul

He's a wonder in my soul

Bless His name.

This song causes me to rejoice because God is so amazing! He never runs short! He never runs out! He always makes a way when there is no way! He does the impossible!!! He's a healer, a provider, a protector, a mind regulator, a burden bearer, and a heavy load sharer!!! He is a wonder to my soul!!! Bless His name!!!!

Contributed by

Jennifer Goldman

Find your favorite version and/or rendition of this song by searching online! Listen to it and celebrate Jesus Christ from your heart and soul! Which version did you listen to? How did it minister to your spirit?

PRAISE REPORT:

_____

_____

_____

_____

_____

_____

_____

_____

_____

_____

_____

_____

_____

_____

_____

DAY 127

Great God

Psalm 95:3--For the LORD is the great God, And the great King above all gods.

PRAISE DAY 127— Psalm 150:1 & 2 tell us to "Praise ye the LORD. Praise God in his sanctuary: praise Him in the firmament of his power. 2) Praise Him for his mighty acts: praise Him according to his excellent greatness."

When we realize how GREAT God is, we know that if He can do all that He has done in creation (Genesis 1), then our petitions, problems and circumstances are NOTHING! Look out into the expanse of the heavens! See the beauty in the stars. Feel the warmth of the sun in the morning! Look around you and see the work of His hands in nature, in space, in you! Everyone, no matter how great or small, can look around and see something beautiful in the world, all over the place. There is evidence of the wonderful works of the Lord all around us!

Today, meditate on how GREAT GOD is! HE created the world and everything in it from NOTHING! He spoke the Word and it manifested! Look at God's nature around you and see—again—how GREAT He is! Praise Him! Praise God our CREATOR, our MAKER! The One who can take NOTHING and make EVERYTHING!

Take time to look at the wonderful works of the Lord today! And praise Him for all that He has created!

PRAISE REPORT:

_____

_____

_____

_____

_____

_____

_____

_____

_____

_____

_____

_____

_____

_____

DAY 128

He Knows My Heart

Psalm 37:4-- Delight yourself also in the LORD,
And He shall give you the desires of your heart.

PRAISE DAY 128—The word "delight" means to enjoy, to be happy. This Scripture tells us to be "happy" and find enjoyment is the Lord, always! It is so easy for us to love the Lord and praise His Name when things are going well in our lives. But, what about when things are not going so well? What about when sickness invades our family or when you and your spouse are going through a divorce? What about when money is low? What about when you are feeling low and depressed?

Sometimes, we feel like the Israelites when they were taken into captivity and their captures asked them to sing songs of Zion. We too find ourselves being held captive by our state of affairs and we feel as if we have been abandoned by God in some strange place. We ask ourselves the question, "How can we sing the Lord's songs in a foreign land (Psalm 137:4)"? How do we "delight" ourselves in the Lord? Simple! Love Jesus more than your circumstances! The evidence in our spiritual growth is exemplified in our ability to thank Him, worship and praise Him continually! It is in our praise that we "delight" ourselves in Him and it is in our enjoyment in Christ Jesus where we will find our blessing! Don't you realize that our praise to God is for our benefit, more than for God's? The Lord promises that He will give us what we desire—providing it is in His will for us—if we simply find enjoyment, peace and happiness in serving Him! Now, praise Him as if you already have what you desire in your heart!

PRAISE REPORT:

_____

_____

_____

_____

_____

_____

_____

_____

_____

_____

_____

_____

_____

_____

_____

DAY 129

He Prepares the Table for Me

Psalm 23:5-- You prepare a table before me in the presence
of my enemies;
You anoint my head with oil;
My cup runs over.

PRAISE DAY 129—We all go through periods where we feel "squeezed" by our conditions in life. We feel like throwing in the towel and just giving up.

Be encouraged today and take your example from a simple balloon! If you take a balloon that is filled to its full capacity with air, it will burst as soon as you put pressure on it. However, if you take the same balloon and partially fill it with air, when you squeeze one side, it increases in another! So, first realize, that if God was to allow you to be full to your capacity, chance are, with only a little pressure, you would burst! Secondly, when God is allowing this "pressure" to come upon you, then you are not "filled to your full potential"! There is still room for you to grow! With that being the case, He will allow the pressure in one area of your life in order to increase you in another! What we are experiencing now is something to prepare us for what God has planned in the future!

Don't worry about people being promoted over you. Don't worry about someone buying the house that you were looking at.

Don't worry about the car that you couldn't buy today. Either it is not for you, or the Lord is using your situation to prepare you for what is to come!

No matter if others get there before we do, what He has prepared for us is only for us! God does not give everybody everything, but He does give everybody *something*!

DON'T GIVE UP--PRAISE REPORT:

_____

_____

_____

_____

_____

_____

_____

_____

_____

_____

_____

_____

_____

_____

DAY 130

God Bless America

Genesis 12:3-- I will bless those who bless you,
And I will curse him who curses you;
And in you all the families of the earth shall be blessed. "

PRAISE DAY 130—"Give me your tired, your poor, Your huddled masses yearning to breathe free, The wretched refuse of your teeming shore. Send these, the homeless, tempest-tossed, to me: I lift my lamp beside the golden door." These are the word quoted by Emma Lazarus. These words have also been engraved on the Statute of Liberty and resonate as a symbol of freedom to those who seek refuge.

The United States of America has been a country for refugees from her beginning. It is only in the last few decades, with terrorism being on the rise that she has had to take a strong look at those who seek asylum in our "freedom lands".

A quick look at Israel's history in the Old Testament would reveal that from the time of Abraham to 1948, the Israelites have been seeking a place to call home. When we look back through history, one can only surmise that the success of the USA can be linked to her embracing the "huddled masses," which included God's people mentioned in Genesis 12:3. Even now, when we entertain strangers, we set ourselves up to be blessed (Hebrews 13:2). So today, as you go through your day, praise God for an opportunity to bless someone you don't even know!

PRAISE REPORT:

_____

_____

_____

_____

_____

_____

_____

_____

_____

_____

_____

_____

_____

_____

_____

_____

_____

DAY 131

Your Will Be Done

Matthew 6:10-- **Your kingdom come.**
Your will be done
On earth as *it is* in heaven.

PRAISE DAY 131— We pray and ask God to direct our lives and we say to Him, "Lord, my life is in Your hands," and we proclaim, "Use me, for I am available to You!" And then, when the Lord puts us in places and circumstances that we find uncomfortable, we wonder what's really going on! When the Lord wants us to do something that is out of our character, we want to be disappointed with Him. We may even feel overwhelmed because of the task that God has placed before us seems so much larger than our own abilities.

There is something we need to know. If God would give you a task that you were able to complete on your own, then it would not be from Him! God places us in situations and gives us assignments that He knows we are incapable of completing on our own because He wants us to rely on Him in order to perform that task that He has ordained!

Has the Lord been placing a yearning in your spirit to do something great? Is that something "Kingdom" worthy? Then submit and surrender to His will in your life! When you pray, "Your kingdom come, Your will be done," you are making a declarative statement, "BE DONE will of God, in my life!" I have heard it said more than once, "If the Lord brings you to it, He will take you through it!" He will not assign you to a task and then not provide you with the resources, skills and wisdom to get the task done.

Search your heart, submit to the will of God and Praise Him for finding you worthy to do the work!

PRAISE REPORT:

_____

_____

_____

_____

_____

_____

_____

_____

_____

_____

_____

_____

_____

DAY 132

Jesus is My Friend

Proverbs 18:24-- A man who has friends must himself be
friendly,

But there is a friend who sticks closer than a
brother.

PRAISE **DAY 132**—If someone was to ask you your
definition of a friend, what would be your reply? Would
you say "companion"? Would you say "someone who
sticks by you no matter what"? Are you blessed to have that one
true friend that you can call in the middle of the night and they
answer your call? Do you have someone close enough to you that
you can tell all of your secrets to without the fear of others finding
out?

If you can't, and even if you can, there is One Friend who is
better than all of your friends put together! This Friend is an ally, a
close companion, a listening ear, a broad shoulder you can cry on,
one you can call on morning noon or night and He's never too busy
to respond to your call! Even though He's my friend, He can and
will be your Friend too!

In the hymn, "There's Not a Friend Like the Lowly Jesus,"
by Johnson Oatman Jr. (1856-1926), we are provided with a good
description of this Friend JESUS! Rejoice in Him today because He

is our friend who sticks closer than any brother. None can heal the way He can. None can touch me the way He can. My situation can never be so dark that He can't console and restore me! He is my/our on time friend! He will never forsake us. Let us praise and worship our Lord and Savior!

He is with you now! What would you tell your Friend Jesus?

PRAISE REPORT:

_____

_____

_____

_____

_____

_____

_____

_____

_____

_____

_____

_____

_____

_____

DAY 133

Joy in the Morning

Psalm 30:5-- For His anger *is but for* a moment,
His favor *is for* life;
Weeping may endure for a night,
But joy *comes* in the morning.

PRAISE DAY 133—There are times when I know that I have done some things that were not in line with God's Word! I'm just like you—human! Christian, yes; human, YES! We all have faults and there will be times when our actions and behavior are displeasing to God. If we are not careful, we will allow those times to cause a separation from Him. When that happens, we are to blame because Jesus promised that no one would be able to snatch us from His hand (John 10:28). However, we can choose to walk away!

This verse of Scripture serves again as encouragement for us. Just as children feel badly when they disappoint their parents, we also feel that we have disappointed our Father in heaven. The thing about this is, WE are the ones who actually feel as if God is angry with us! Don't get stuck there in "anger" zone! Read the next sentence that tells us His favor is for life.

The first two sentences are in comparison to the second two sentences. His anger to our weeping; His favor to our joy!

When you fall short of God's glory, you won't fall out of His grace and you will not out live His favor! Weeping may endure for a night—which is for just a moment—but dry your weeping eyes because His joy is coming in the morning! Rejoice and be exceedingly glad!

PRAISE & JOY REPORT:

_____

_____

_____

_____

_____

_____

_____

_____

_____

_____

_____

_____

_____

DAY 134

Come and See

Acts 3:8, 9-- So he, leaping up, stood and walked and entered the temple with them—walking, leaping, and praising God. 9) And all the people saw him walking and praising God

PRAISE DAY 134—If you have ever been to a ball game, you can probably remember the excitement and energy that filled the place where you were! You can remember your favorite plays, even the ones where your team didn't score. The play may have been so dramatic or dynamic that it is forever impressed on your mind. It, above anything else, is the one thing you continue to share with whoever will listen, even years after the game has been played.

One of the Bible stories that I enjoy reading and sharing is the one about the man at the Gate called Beautiful who was healed (Acts chapter 3). As Peter and John were walking into the temple they saw the man who, as Scripture points out, was lame from birth. Everyone knew he was lame and he was allowed to sit by the temple and beg for money.

Peter and John were quick to respond to the man in a manner he was not expecting, but it was the manner that he needed. They said to him, "Silver and gold I do not have, but what I do have I give you: In the name of Jesus Christ of Nazareth, rise up and walk." The man immediately was healed! As a result of his healing, he stood up, walking around, leaping and praising God! That is the same type of excitement all Believers should have and it is an excitement that we should readily share with others.

Invite an unchurched person to attend church with you this week! What are you afraid of? Pray! Allow the Lord to prepare someone for you to invite to church! Write down their names and pray for them. Then, praise the Lord for their salvation!

Tools specific to Act 3:9

Act 3:9

.

PRAISE REPORT:

_____

_____

_____

_____

_____

_____

_____

_____

_____

_____

_____

DAY 135

God, My Father

Psalm 68:5-- A father of the fatherless, a defender of
    widows,
    Is God in His holy habitation.

PRAISE DAY 135—Let's face it! There are just too many fatherless households in America today. There was a time in our culture that fathers were the head of the house and the home. Where there was not father, generally, there were no children. The family was the first institution created by God in the book of Genesis. There was Adam, the father; Eve, the mother; and the children, Cain, Abel and Seth.

Even in the New Testament, in Ephesians 5:25, the husband is the one who is commanded to "love"! The wife is told to submit and the children are told to obey. Love comes from the father, down. The husband/father is instructed to love his wife and family, be responsible to the wife and children, just as we expect Christ to be the head of our churches.

With fathers being so absent in the family, it is a delight to know that God is still our heavenly Father! He sees all and He knows all. He cares for us, loves us, protects and provides for us! We can and we do pray, "Our Father which is in heaven."

Let us take this time to praise God for being our Father! Not only that, but pray for the men that you know who are stepping up to the task of being an earthly father example for children everywhere! Pray for the fatherless children. Pray that God will send them someone who will love them like a father should and pray that these children come to know the Father for themselves! Praise Him for being our Father in Heaven!

PRAISE FOR FATHERS:

_____

_____

_____

_____

_____

_____

_____

_____

_____

_____

_____

_____

_____

_____

_____

DAY 136

God's Promotion

Psalm 75:6, 7-- **For promotion [cometh] neither from the east, nor from the west, nor from the south. 7) But God [is] the judge: he putteth down one, and setteth up another. (KJV)**

PRAISE DAY 136— Your promotion is at hand! Give God the PRAISE! Know that it is He who promotes you; it is He who delivers you, it is He who makes your enemies your footstool! What do you believe God for? Your increase comes from God and not man! Don't depend on man to uplift you or exalt you or promote your, or increase you!

Even if God has to move someone out of the way or create a position just for you, He can and He will—exalt you when you humble yourself. So, this day, surrender your service as unto the Lord! What God has for you, it is for you and no one can undo what God has done! HE will open doors that cannot be shut. HE will close doors that cannot be opened! So, PRAISE HIM today for everything HE has for you according to His PERFECT will! In Jesus' Name we pray and praise!!

PRAISE REPORT:

_____

_____

_____

_____

_____

_____

_____

_____

_____

_____

_____

_____

_____

_____

_____

_____

_____

_____

DAY 137

A Day to Surrender

Romans 12:15-- Rejoice with them that do rejoice, and weep with them that weep.

PRAISE DAY 137— A Day to surrender. There are times when mourning is necessary. Even in our praise, take time to mourn. Not only do we mourn for ourselves but, for others also. We may not be able to feel what others who are hurting may feel, but we can still mourn. We can take a moment and cry with them. We can take a moment and share in their agony. We can take time out of our day and sympathize. When we do, let us also surrender! Yes, we can worship God when we surrender ALL to HIM!

We know that He can HANDLE ALL that we might come up against! While we are worshipping God and increasing our praise and our faith, the enemy will attack us to get us off balance and to get us off focus. It's okay! Stop! Take a moment, breath, and surrender all of your hurts, all of your pain, all of your sorrows, all of your bad days, and all of your tears, in a moment of SURRENDERED PRAISE! Let the healing begin!

PRAISE REPORT:

_____

_____

_____

_____

_____

_____

_____

_____

_____

_____

_____

_____

_____

_____

_____

_____

_____

_____

_____

_____

DAY 138

My Strength and Redeemer

Psalm 19:14-- Let the words of my mouth, and the meditation of my heart, be acceptable in thy sight, O LORD, my strength, and my redeemer.

PRAISE DAY 138—Watch what you say! Your words become your reality! According to Proverbs 18:2, "Death and life *are* in the power of the tongue, and those who love it will eat its fruit." In other words, we become what we speak! What are you saying about yourself and your circumstances today? What are you saying about your future? How many of your dreams have you killed because of your words? Do your words lift up or do they destroy? Are they bitter or sweet? Are they found in the confines of your own selfishness or are they rooted in the Word of God?

Our words have power to heal, to kill, to destroy or to grow and uplift. Therefore, surrender the power of your own words and allow the Lord to guide, lead, instruct and govern your words. There is a saying that goes, "Think before you speak." Before you speak, THINK:

> **T** - is it True?
> **H** - is it Helpful?
> **I** - is it Inspiring?
> **N** - is it Necessary?
> **K** - is it Kind?

Using this thinking/speaking pattern in our lives will help us to only speak those things that God will be pleased with. He is our strength and our power. He is our redeemer, our liberator, rescuer, and our knight in shining armor!

As you go through your day today, only speak those things that are positive, those things that are true and uplifting.

PRAISE REPORT:

_____

_____

_____

_____

_____

_____

_____

_____

_____

_____

_____

_____

_____

_____

_____

DAY 139

He Keeps My Mind

Isaiah 26:3— You will keep him in perfect peace, Whose mind is stayed on You, Because he trusts in You.

PRAISE DAY 139—Something I learned in Psychology 101, in college, that I will have a hard time forgetting. I can't remember my professor's name, but I do remember what he said. He explained that, "Nobody can make you angry! You choose whether or not you are going to be angry or not!" From that, we learned that in violent situations where the assailant says, "You made me mad!" as their justification for violence, they are merely shifting the blame from themselves onto their victim!

Later in my adult life, I realized that situations are neutral. The way respond to them, we choose to do so in either a positive, negative or neutral manner. For example, in a vehicle accident you have several choices in your response. 1) NEGATIVE--You can choose to get out of your car and yell and blame the other driver for the accident; 2) POSTIVE--you can choose to get out of your car and go to check on the other persons to make sure they are okay and call for assistance; or 3) NEUTRAL--you can choose not to do anything except get out of your car, move out of danger and call the police.

As Christians, it becomes important in our walk that we always respond in a positive manner to every situation that we many encounter. The verse above tells us to keep our minds on the Lord and He will keep our minds in a state of peace. I have three words to help you with this: DON'T LOSE FOCUS! Let me say that again! Don't lose focus, DON'T lose focus! DON'T LOSE focus! DON'T, DON'T lose Focus!! Praise Him! DON''T you DARE LOSE YOUR FOCUS! (Satan, get behind me, in Jesus' Name!) DON'T LOSE FOCUS!!!!!

PRAISE REPORT:

_____

_____

_____

_____

_____

_____

_____

_____

_____

_____

_____

_____

_____

_____

DAY 140

Blessings Come to the Righteous

Psalm 1:1 -- Blessed *is* the man
Who walks not in the counsel of the ungodly,
Nor stands in the path of sinners,
Nor sits in the seat of the scornful;

PRAISE DAY 140—The Book of Psalms opens with the verse above. The first few words of that portion of Scripture start out by saying that man is blessed! Then, the conditions of being blessed are listed in the next few stanzas. To be blessed, you have to avoid seeking and receiving advice from ungodly people, be removed for the paths of sinners (don't go in the same way, doing the same things that ungodly people do), and refuse to sit in a place where you are disrespectful and making fun of other people. Additionally, as recorded in verse 2, you have to appreciate the Word of God so much that you obey the Word, you live the Word, and you share the Word with an enormous degree of excitement!

It's no doubt that every one of us wants to be blessed. We speak about the blessings of God all the time. Pastors have built ministries on the foundation of God's innumerable blessings. However, a huge shadow is sometimes cast over the requirements or the prerequisites for receiving the blessing of God. The requirements are listed in verses one and two. The blessing or benefits are listed in verse three as follows:

> **He shall be like a tree**
> **Planted by the rivers of water,**
> **That brings forth its fruit in its season,**
> **Whose leaf also shall not wither;**
> **And whatever he does shall prosper.**

Did you get that last part? Whatsoever he does shall prosper! That lets me know and encourages me that whatever I do will prosper if I love and obey the Word of God, if I put God first in everything that I do and first in everything I hope for! If I am putting God first, then I also put Him first when it comes to my desires. I pray that my desires will line up with His Word and His will for me! Trust God, obey Him and be blessed!

PRAISE REPORT:

_____

_____

_____

_____

_____

_____

_____

_____

_____

_____

_____

DAY 141

The Lord is My Avenger

Psalm 37:1, 2—*A Psalm* of David.
Do not fret because of evildoers,
Nor be envious of the workers of iniquity. 2) For
they shall soon be cut down like the grass,
And wither as the green herb.

PRAISE DAY 141—Have you ever looked around and noticed how some wealthy people can seem to have it all? But, at the same time, they seem to be so miserable. What about people who commit evil against you? If we are not careful, we will allow the evildoers to interfere with our praise and our purpose.

It is not for us to wonder when and/if "they will get what's coming to them". Our duty is to forgive and let go. Forgiveness is a tool that we Christians can use in order to free us from the burden of strife, agony and misery that stems from some villain. When we fail to forgive, we imprison ourselves! We feel weighted down, depressed and miserable when the wrongdoer is going on about his or her life.

We should be encouraged today, knowing that God sees, He hears, He knows and He cares! Psalm 37:6 says, "He shall bring forth your righteousness as the light, and your justice as the noonday." Let the Lord take care of your enemies, as you wait on Him! For it is then that you/we shall inherit the earth (Psalm 37:9).

The Lord is our Avenger! Psalm 37:13 tells us how the Lord sees the malefactors. It says, "The Lord laughs at him, for He sees that his day is coming." The Lord knows already what is in store for those who are workers of iniquity against us! Rest; knowing that God has the matters against you in His proficient hands! Since you now know, go ahead; Give God some Praise!

PRAISE REPORT:

_____

_____

_____

_____

_____

_____

_____

_____

_____

_____

_____

_____

_____

_____

_____

_____

_____

_____

_____

_____

DAY 142

Thank God for Salvation

I Chronicles 16:23—Sing to the LORD, all the earth;
Proclaim the good news of His salvation from day to
day.

PRAISE DAY 142—I just want to take this opportunity to praise God for salvation! He is everything to me! I am complete in Him. I have the promise of everlasting life, if I just believe that He is and accept Him as Ruler and King in my life. I praise Him for removing everything from my life that does not draw me closer to Him.

He helps me to focus on the things that are eternal. I am so thankful for His everlasting love. His joy and peace have no end. He helps me to focus on those things and He helps me to trust Him for everything I need physically and spiritually. He is in control of my body, He is in control of my life and He is in control of my spirit! I trust Him with every breath I take, knowing that when I go to sleep at night I rest in His bosom. And, if He sees fit, He will wake me up in the morning! When I take my last breath on this side, I will wake up in His presence!

He is my God, my Savior and my Father. He loves me and wants me to spend eternity with Him. No other god comes close to the One true and living God. He is faithful, even unto death! I thank Him for being here for me!

Contributed by Ethel "Mother" Ellis

PRAISE REPORT:

_____

_____

_____

_____

_____

_____

_____

_____

_____

_____

_____

_____

_____

_____

_____

_____

_____

_____

DAY 143

Lead Me to the Rock

Ps. 61:1-4, 8— Hear my cry, O God, Attend unto my prayer.

From the end of the earth will I cry unto thee, when my heart is overwhelmed : Lead me to the tock that is higher than I. For thou hast been a shelter for me, and a strong tower from the enemy. I will abide in Thy tabernacle forever. I will trust in the cover of thy wings. So will I sing praise unto Thy name forever, that I may daily perform my vows. KJV

PRAISE DAY 143— In life we have many challenges. At times, we are able to handle them. Other times, our challenges are or seem so much larger than we are. These challenges may consume us. We wake up with them; we go throughout the day with them; we lie down with them only to rise up with them in the morning and start all over with them again. We all have had times when we cried out for God to hear us and attend to our needs or take action on our behalf. Yet, He seems so far away. In instances such as these, we generally turn to others.

Sometimes, we turn to someone who will have a pity party with us. We provide the cake and ice cream; they bring the balloons and confetti. Other times, we turn to someone to tell us that we should take actions that we know are not of God, but it will make us feel so good for the moment. Still, often times we turn to others to vent until we have analyzed the challenge and others, inside out, upside down and round and round. May I add that we even may use a combination of all of these? However we have chosen to handle our challenges, there are times when we find ourselves at the end of the earth, others and ourselves crying out to our LORD.

During these times, it is important that we run to those who will lead us to the rock that is higher than I. These persons will remind us that we have a source that is strong and able to anchor us in when the storms of life are raging. We need someone who will tell us that the challenge is larger than them, but there is One who is higher than I and He is the rock of our salvation. He is the source and strength of our life and that He will do anything but fail us. Why do we need to be reminded of this?

Because we will begin to remember that in the times of storms, He has been a shelter for us. We will remember that He is a strong tower from the enemy and that no weapon formed against us shall prosper, not because we are right or have done everything right. It is because of His mercy and grace towards us that He looks beyond our faults and meets our every need whether we are right or wrong. As we remember and experience His love, we will want to abide in the tabernacle of that love forever knowing that He is taking us from faith to faith and from glory to glory. We can boldly say, "I will trust in the covert of Thy wings" and then pause to think about it for a moment. Why under His wings?

I saw a geographic story on television some time back of some fire fighters fighting a forest fire. They came across what appeared to be a scorched bird, lying on the ground with its wings spread. One of the fire fighters kicked the bird over and to everyone's surprise baby chicks ran from underneath the bird with no evidence of ever being in the fire. The fire fighters began to shout for joy and take pictures. Truly, if His is eye is on the sparrow, we can hide under the protection of His wings in times of challenges and know that He is willing to die for our protection. He will not let this challenge destroy us.

Take some time to begin to write down some of the past and present blessings of God giving Him praise for each one and then.......perform your daily duties with joy and assurance that we serve a God who is more than able to do exceedingly and abundantly above all we may ask or think. Have a blessed day!!!!

Contributed by Minister Bernita Taylor

PRAISE REPORT:

_____

_____

_____

_____

_____

_____

_____

_____

_____

_____

_____

_____

_____

_____

_____

_____

_____

_____

_____

_____

_____

_____

DAY 144
Praise in Times of Trouble

Psalm 27:5-- **For in the time of trouble**
He shall hide me in His pavilion;
In the secret place of His tabernacle
He shall hide me;
He shall set me high upon a rock.

PRAISE DAY 18—One Sunday morning I preached to an almost empty sanctuary! The only people there were my daughter, a deacon and me! Nevertheless, my topic was "Thanks God, in Everything!" from I Thessalonians 5:16-18. We understand why evil people are punished, but our greatest controversy is in trying to understand why "good" people suffer.

Well, if Noah had his ark, Abraham had his test, Jeremiah was thrown in a cistern (out house), Job lost all that he had, David had his Goliath, Daniel had his lion's den, Elijah had his Jezebel, Elisha died even though he brought a young boy back to life, and JESUS had his Cross!! What makes you think you are so special, so holy, so righteous that you won't have your burdens to bear and endure! God commands us, through Paul, to Give Thanks IN (not for, but IN) everything! So as I was preaching to the walls, the pews, my daughter and the deacon, the words of the message also began to resonate in my spirit!! God will not take to you a place of failure--it may seem like it is, but when you look a little closer, you will realize it is a test! , Jeremiah trusted God and bought property, Job received double of what he had lost, David became king, Daniel became a ruler in a foreign land, Elijah was taken up to Glory in a chariot of fire, Elisha died a great prophet of God, and JESUS had rose from the dead with all power in His hands!! Before the victory, there has to be a battle, before the triumph, there has to be a test! So, no matter where you are in your life right now, Thank GOD in your situation, knowing that He sees you and He cares!! Then, get ready to step into your blessing!!! I pray that this brief summary has blessed you today, in Jesus' Name!!!

PRAISE REPORT:

_____

_____

_____

_____

_____

_____

_____

_____

_____

_____

DAY 145

Praise is My Weapon

Psalm 149:6, 7-- Let the High praises of God be in their
mouth, and a two-edged sword in their hand;

PRAISE **DAY 145**—The Bible gives us two spiritual
weapons. The sword mentioned in Ephesians 6:17b—
"and the sword of the Spirit, which is the word of God,"
is one that we all may be familiar with. There is a weapon
mentioned in Psalm 144:6b. This verse identifies our weapon as a
sword of praise! There are several Biblical examples where praise
has been used effectively as a weapon against the enemy.

In the book of Joshua, praise was used to break the stronghold
(the walls) of Jericho.

- As believers, we can have strongholds that we need to be
  delivered from.
- We only have to receive salvation once. However, we can be
  delivered many times from many things, all of them having
  their origin in sin/Satan.
  - ~ We pray, "deliver us from evil"
  - ~ We pray, "lead us not into temptation but
    deliver us from evil."

The children of Israel sanctified themselves before they

went over into Canaan to face their enemy (Joshua 3:5). As a result, there was no fear in the Israelites when they stood against the city and people of Jericho .

As Christians, there are several things we need to be aware of.

- You have to sanctify yourself before you can use praise against your enemy.
- Your enemy shows up when you "cross over"
- Victory is already yours!
- You can use praise when you are obedient go God! Without obedience, our praise is in vain. God gave Israel victory because of their obedience to praise Him!

In Jonah 2:9 and 10, Jonah found himself in the dangerous position of being in the belly of the great fish for three days and three nights. When he offered up a sacrifice of praise, prayer and thanksgiving, he was delivered out of his treacherous circumstance. And again in I Samuel 16:23, it reads, "And so it was, whenever the spirit from God was upon Saul, that David would take a harp and play *it* with his hand. Then Saul would become refreshed and well, and the distressing spirit would depart from him". David used praise to chase away an evil spirit.

The next time you feel a distressing spirit or when you need to be delivered from a stronghold, shout your way through, shout your way out with praise! If it is not you, but someone else who needs to be delivered, you become their "David" and that person becomes your "Saul"! You have probably been praying for that person, perhaps for years, so now praise the Lord for their deliverance!

PRAISE IS A WEAPON:

_____

_____

_____

_____

_____

_____

_____

_____

_____

_____

_____

_____

_____

_____

_____

_____

_____

DAY 146
Praise Him With the Hymns

Colossians 3:16-- Let the word of Christ dwell in you richly in all wisdom; teaching and admonishing one another in psalms and hymns and spiritual songs, singing with grace in your hearts to the Lord.

PRAISE DAY 146— In life we have many trials and troubles. The thing about trouble is that it comes wrapped up in just my size! Trouble knows my name and yours. Trouble knows exactly what will bother me and what will bother you. Trouble knows where we live and just when we least expect it, trouble comes knocking at our door.

At times, we are able to hide the fact that trouble has paid us a visit. We continue to go through our day, pretending as if all is well when on the inside we are crying intensely. We go through our day, anxiously waiting for the clock on the wall to indicate it is time to go home, where we once more, come face to face with trouble.

This verse in Colossians encourages us to lift up one another, with praise, singing hymns and spiritual songs that will uplift our hearts. One of my favorite hymns that uplifts me in every situation is "Father, I Stretch My Hands to Thee," written by Charles Wesley. Wesley wrote over 600 hymns before his death in 1788. Of those he has written, the previously mentioned one is listed among my favorites.

Hymns remain an encouraging facet in our relationship with Christ, even today! Where gospels songs may come and go the hymns remain! Today, sing one of your favorite hymns, allowing it to resonate in your spirit and encouraging your heart! Sing out loud! Someone else around you will also be blessed!

PRAISE WITH THE HYMNS:

_____

_____

_____

_____

_____

_____

_____

_____

_____

_____

_____

_____

_____

DAY 147

Praise Him in the Dance

Psalm 150:4-- For Praise Him with the timbrel and dance;
Praise Him with stringed instruments and flutes!

PRAISE DAY 147—I really enjoy dancing! When I was a younger and in college, I would go out sometimes with friends and other times I would go alone. Where young girls my age would want to go out to find a man or to get a date, I just wanted to have some fun.

When I became serious in my walk with Christ, my "clubbing days" were over! However, I still enjoy dancing! As the saying goes, "I haven't stopped dancing, I just changed partners." Singing praises to God can be beneficial, but praising Him in the dance is most liberating!

Others may think that dancing is drastic and shouldn't be part of church worship. Sometimes, your radical praise will cause others some discomfort. They may disapprove of your ability to express yourself in your praise and worship to God. They will want you to sit down, be quiet and be reverent. The pious people will want you to be removed from them and will beckon for ushers to escort you out of the church. Others will claim to be embarrassed by your open show of affection and gratification to God, just as

David's wife, Michal, was upset with him and his radical praise to God (II Samuel 6:15).

The next time you are in your church service, be encouraged to express yourself in the praise and the dance! Or, if you are just too shy to dance at church, put on your praise music and praise the Lord in the dance in your home! Once you get into the practice in private, you will be more than willing to let go and praise God in the dance in public! Below, share your "praise dance" experience!

PRAISE HIM IN THE DANCE:

_____

_____

_____

_____

_____

_____

_____

_____

_____

_____

_____

DAY 148

God Inhabits My Praise

Psalm 22:3-- But You *are* holy,
Enthroned in the praises of Israel.

PRAISE DAY 148—You may have wondered and asked yourself the question, "Why a praise journal?" The answer is quite simple. Prayer journals have been around for years! I have taught courses on the subject of prayer for many years. I have found that many Christians pray and do so unceasingly. But, I have also found that many of their prayers go unanswered! This leaves Christians in a state of confusion and despair. Strong Christians become weak and weary of all their praying. Praying is easy; waiting on the answer may be a long tormenting process—to some. This book is to encourage all Christians, regardless of the strength of their faith, to praise God while waiting! Stop focusing so much on the problem but praising God for His promises!

The main reason to encourage people of God to praise is found in the verse above. God "shows up" when we praise! Prayers and prayer requests have a tendency to change with the wind! Through the prayer journals I have read, as part of the course requirements for students who participated in my classes, the prayer requests of the students changed so much that some of the requests even contradicted others! This, of course, was a lesson that I wanted to make clear to the students. Sometimes God can't move on what we have prayed for because a few days later we pray in the opposite direction!

Praises to God, on the other hand, is praise to Him no matter how often or by what process we choose to praise Him. Psalm 150 gives us a wide assortment of ways to praise God! We can praise Him on instruments, praise with songs—there are so many songs to choose from, praise Him with our hand—uplifted, waving, outstretched, we can praise Him with dancing! Praise is exhilarating and liberating!

One of my favorite Biblical examples of God's presence in praise is found in II Chronicles 5:11-14, which reads: —

> *And it came to pass when the priests came out of the Most Holy Place (for all the priests who were present had sanctified themselves, without keeping to their divisions), 12) and the Levites who were the singers, all those of Asaph and Heman and Jeduthun, with their sons and their brethren, stood at the east end of the altar, clothed in white linen, having cymbals, stringed instruments and harps, and with them one hundred and twenty priests sounding with trumpets, 13) indeed it came to pass, when the trumpeters and singers were as one, to make one sound to be heard in praising and thanking the*

LORD, and when they lifted up their voice with the trumpets and cymbals and instruments of music, and praised the LORD, saying: "For He is good, For His mercy endures forever," that the house, the house of the LORD, was filled with a cloud, 14) so that the priests could not continue ministering because of the cloud; for the glory of the LORD filled the house of God.

This story provides vivid evidence regarding the positive results of our praise and worship of God. The King James Version of this verse is, "But thou art holy, O thou that inhabitest the praises of Israel." This verse plainly tells us that God inhabits the praises of His people! Although we know that our prayers are stored in heaven (Revelation 5:8; Revelation 8:3, 4), it is in our praise that we experience the presence of the Spirit of God! If you want God to show up in your life, then give Him praise!

Workers want what they can get from God. Worshippers want what God can get from them. Are you a worker or a worshipper? Read Psalm 150. Below, write out your "praise commitment" to the Lord!

PRAISE HIM:

_____

_____

_____

_____

_____

_____

_____

_____

_____

_____

_____

_____

_____

_____

_____

_____

_____

DAY 149

Praise Him for His Mighty Acts

Psalm 150:2-- **Praise Him for His mighty acts;
Praise Him according to His excellent greatness!**

PRAISE DAY 149—The Bible starts out with this powerful verse, "In the beginning God created the heavens and the earth." Then chapter 1 in Genesis continues with every Word proceeding out of the mouth of God, calling things into existence. He says in verse 11, "Then God said, "Let the earth bring forth grass, the herb *that* yields seed, *and* the fruit tree *that* yields fruit according to its kind, whose seed *is* in itself, on the earth"; and it was so."

And, in verse 20, "Let the waters abound with an abundance of living creatures, and let birds fly above the earth across the face of the firmament of the heavens." In verse 24, God said, "Let the earth bring forth the living creature according to its kind: cattle and creeping thing and beast of the earth, *each* according to its kind"; and it was so.

As if that wasn't enough to be classified as a "mighty act", think on this; When God said those words in Genesis, He did not indicate that the power of His Words would stop! What?? The earth is still bringing forth animals and plants! Search the web for "newly discovered plants and/or animals" and be amazed by what you find! Every bit of God's Word is just as powerful today as it was and is when He spoke, beginning with Genesis 1:1! We can praise Him for His mighty acts, amazing and wonderful works that constantly reminds us that He is GOD!

PRAISE HIS MIGHTY ACTS:

_____

_____

_____

_____

_____

_____

_____

_____

_____

_____

_____

_____

_____

_____

DAY 150

God Answers Prayer

Psalm 120:1-- A Song of Ascents.

In my distress I cried to the LORD,

And He heard me.

PRAISE **DAY 150**—There have been so many, many times in my life where I have cried out to the Lord and He heard me! From needing food for my children, to a new job, to a new car, to His intervention when I found myself in trouble on the job, God has heard my voice and has responded to my cry.

Having faith includes believing that when you pray, you already have what you have been praying for! Angels are already dispersed to bring your prayer into manifestation. It has already been said, while you are waiting, praise Him! Not only praise Him, but do so in a manner that says you believe the Lord heard your voice!

Write down that one prayer in your life that God answered and you were reassured that He hears and answers your prayers! Now, praise Him for answering every other prayer that you have prayed, in accordance with His word and in His will for your life! He is still in the prayer answering business!

PRAISE HIM FOR ANSWERED PRAYERS:

The Benediction

God is Able

Ephesians 3:20, 21-- "Now to Him who is able to do exceedingly abundantly above all that we ask or think, according to the power that works in us, to Him be glory in the church by Christ Jesus to all generations, forever and ever. Amen.

I close this book with this benediction:

May the blessing of the Lord overtake you, even as you pursue Him. May His grace ever abound in your life. May His mercy be never-ending and His love be ever-flowing. May He bless you with His favor. Keep the lamp of your life held high, for there are many who follow your light!

"Now to Him who is able to do exceedingly abundantly above all that we ask or think, according to the power that works in us, to Him be glory in the church by Christ Jesus to all generations, forever and ever. Amen." (Ephesians 3:20, 21).

Now, shout and give God a praise that counts, then close the book and start again on Day 1....in the morning!

www.ingramcontent.com/pod-product-compliance
Lightning Source LLC
Chambersburg PA
CBHW060002100426
42740CB00010B/1374